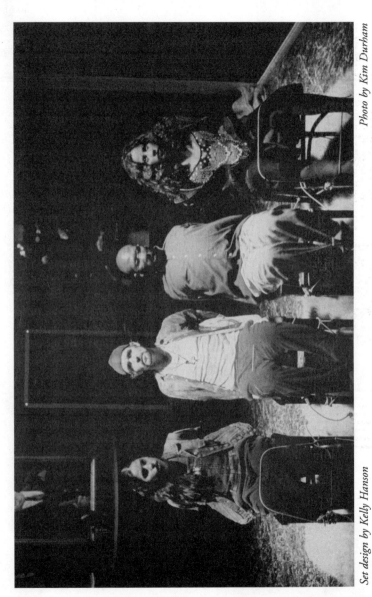

A scene from the Los Angeles revival of *Den of Thieves*.

DEN OF THIEVES

BY STEPHEN ADLY GUIRGIS

★

★

DRAMATISTS
PLAY SERVICE
INC.

For Max Daniels,
who helped me get started
when I was getting ready
to get ready to get started.

THIEVES was first presented by The LAByrinth Theater (Philip Seymour Hoffman and Jon Ortiz, Artistic Directors; Oliver Dow, Executive Director) at HERE in New York City, opening on April 10, 1996. It was directed by Max Daniels; the set design was by Dana Heffern; the lighting design was by Douglas Cox; the costume design was by Daniel Youmans; and the producer/production stage manager was Alex Molina. The cast was as follows:

MAGGIE	Liza Colon-Zayas
PAUL	Chris McGarry
FLACO	Sam Rockwell
BOOCHIE	Lidia Ramirez
SAL	Lou Moreno
LITTLE TUNA	David Zayas
BIG TUNA	Ernest Mingione

The production was later transferred to the Theater Row Theater by the H.A.I. Theater Festival (Michael John Spencer, Producer) with Trevor Long as Flaco and Stephen Adly Guirgis as Sal.

DEN OF THIEVES was revived by The Black Dahlia Theater (Matt Shakman, Artistic Director; Brian Siegel, Managing Director; Maggie Malone, Producing Director) in Los Angeles, California, opening on April 13, 2002. It was directed by Matt Shakman; the set design was by Kelly Hanson; the lighting design was by Mike Durst; the sound design was by Rob Geary; the costume design was by Angelina Burnett; and the production stage manager was Jennifer Welsh. The cast was as follows:

MAGGIE	Ana Ortiz
PAUL	Russell G. Jones
FLACO	Trevor Long
BOOCHIE	Elizabeth Rodriguez
SAL	Bruno Gioiello
LITTLE TUNA	Marco Greco
BIG TUNA	Ronald Hunter

CHARACTERS

MAGGIE

PAUL

FLACO

SAL

BOOCHIE

LITTLE TUNA

BIG TUNA

method everything I do.

Ob: 1 line
answer
for every
thing

[handwritten: — I want to save her.]
[handwritten: — know my facts]
[handwritten: flunar from suft. make serious]

DEN OF THIEVES

[handwritten: — Lecture, preach]

ACT ONE

Maggie's apartment. Maggie is in tears; Paul is doing his utmost to be supportive.

MAGGIE. I feel so stupid right now —
PAUL. — It's okay.
MAGGIE. I mean, this is so *dumb* —
PAUL. — It's not dumb!
MAGGIE. I'm sorry Paul; I don't think I can do this —
PAUL. — Maggie, let me tell you, I've been right where you are right now, and it's hard! It's hard to reach out! It's hard to own up!
MAGGIE. Paul —
PAUL. — You're brave … Don't look at me like that! *You are brave.* Let me ask you something: Is this the first time you've shoplifted since you entered the program?
MAGGIE. Yeah?
PAUL. You haven't stolen anything up till now?
MAGGIE. Not since I entered the program.
PAUL. And when did you go to your first program meeting?
MAGGIE. Two Sundays ago.
PAUL. And tonight you stole?
MAGGIE. I did, I stole! —
PAUL. And then you came home and immediately called a fellow program member and reached out!
MAGGIE. Well, you left your number on my machine —
PAUL. — And you used it! The first time you stole, you reached out!
MAGGIE. But —

[handwritten: Point out]

7

PAUL. — I gotta tell you, I've been theft-free for 682 days now, but I stole like a dozen times before I was ever brave enough to reach out. And you, you did it the very first time!

MAGGIE. You've been theft-free 682 days? What's it feel like?

PAUL. Feels like one day at a time, Maggie.

MAGGIE. … I, I'm scared Paul, I can't hardly speak, I got a big lump in my throat

PAUL. Hey, the first time I did what you're about to do, I had a big lump too.

MAGGIE. Yeah?

PAUL. I had a SNIB.

MAGGIE. SNIB?

PAUL. Spontaneous Nerve-Induced Bowel-Movement. I pooped my pants.

MAGGIE. You what? —

PAUL. Hey, I thank my Higher Power every day for that SNIB 'cuz I gotta tell you : I was afraid to *reach out* just like you; I wanted to *hold it all in,* and my Higher Power, he knew that, and so "He did for me what I could not do for myself:" He forced me to let it out, and believe me, I "let it out" … God has a plan for us all, Maggie. For me, it was that I should defecate in my favorite pair of slacks. For you, it's that you're here, right now, with me … So … Here we go, the big moment of truth! Are you ready?

MAGGIE. I guess.

PAUL. Okay … So, where is it?

MAGGIE. What?

PAUL. Whatever you stole. Where is it?

MAGGIE. In my bag here.

PAUL. … So What did you steal, Maggie? *(Maggie opens the bag, takes out Yodels.)* Yodels. Okay You stole Yodels. *(She takes out toothpaste.)* Toothpaste. Okay, you stole Yodels and toothpaste. *(She takes out more stuff.)* Aged parmesan cheese, pesto sauce, room freshener … What's this?

MAGGIE. I'm not sure. Some kind of fruit. *(A lot more stuff spills out.)*

PAUL. Two tomatoes.

MAGGIE. Eight ninety-nine a pound! Can you believe it?

PAUL. Who's robbing who, huh? … So, is that it? *(Maggie empties*

8

bag, many products spill out.) That's quite a haul; you must be good —
MAGGIE. There's more. *(She empties her pockets.)*
PAUL. Is that it?
MAGGIE. Um …
PAUL. It's okay. Show me what else.
MAGGIE. Oh God —
PAUL. Hey, it's okay.
MAGGIE. I stole this change purse from that old lady in the wheelchair who was sitting next to me at the meeting tonight.
PAUL. Willamina?
MAGGIE. I don't know what came over me. She was so sweet and supportive and nurturing — and I stole from her; that sweet old lady —
PAUL. — Hey, she did eight years in Attica for armed robbery, she wasn't always sweet.
MAGGIE. For real?
PAUL. She was only paroled six months ago.
MAGGIE. I don't know how I'll face her.
PAUL. You'll face her … So, anything else?
MAGGIE. You got a cigarette?
PAUL. Don't smoke. Not for 348 days.
MAGGIE. Paul?
PAUL. Yes.
MAGGIE. Here.
PAUL. That's my…! You stole my wallet?
MAGGIE. I'm *deeply* sorry.
PAUL. How'd you steal my wallet?
MAGGIE. Remember on the elevator?
PAUL. What?
MAGGIE. I brushed up against you?
PAUL. I thought you were flirting.
MAGGIE. I wasn't.
PAUL. Wow! I must be slipping.
MAGGIE. No, I'm just good. *(Beat.)*
PAUL. Can I ask you something?
MAGGIE. What?
PAUL. Do you think it's possible that by stealing my wallet you were maybe, I dunno, subconsciously trying to get my attention?

9

'Cuz I mean, I've seen you staring at me before, tonight even —

MAGGIE. — I was starin' at the money you were counting at the beginning of the meeting — it looked like a lot of money.

PAUL. Damn, I am slipping: flashing my wad in a room full of fuckin' kleptos! I mean, Maggie, don't get me wrong —

MAGGIE. — No, you're right.

PAUL. No I'm not! I am wrong and I need to make an amends to you immediately! I apologize … See, that's the *old* me that made that "klepto" remark. The *new* me wants to trust. And I'm working to trust One Day at a Time. I trust you, Maggie. I want you to know that. You stole my wallet, but than you returned it, no harm, no foul. *(He looks inside the wallet.)* Where's my fucking money?!

MAGGIE. I'll pay you back —

PAUL. Pay me back?! Just give it back.

MAGGIE. They were gonna kick me outta here, Paul — I needed it for rent!

PAUL. I had 800 bucks in there! I was planning to attend a holistic wellness retreat in Vail, Colorado!

MAGGIE. Look. I got a TV, some stereo equipment, I got a new microwave. Take it! Take all of it! I'm a fuck-up, I don't belong in the program! I thought I did but I don't. I'm incurable. I'm sorry, Paul.

PAUL. Maggie —

MAGGIE. — No! I gave this self-help thing a try. I went to meetings, got my "chakra's aligned"; I became real familiar with the personal growth section of Barnes & Noble. I tried, and I'll never be better, I'll always be like this! I'm a bad person and I can't be saved, and even if I could, I'm not worthy of a better life, I'm not worthy of anything! I'm going to bed now! Take what you want, just, leave the food and close the door behind you. *(Maggie picks up the Yodels from the pile of stolen goods and starts heading for her bedroom.)*

PAUL. Maggie!

MAGGIE. Goodbye, Paul.

PAUL. Put the Yodels down, Maggie!

MAGGIE. What?

PAUL. Gimme the Yodels.

MAGGIE. No!

PAUL. Maggie, you don't wanna eat those!

MAGGIE. Yes I do! … And I want that Heathbar too!

10

Don't Play Humor

PAUL. You can't have the Heathbar, Maggie!

MAGGIE. Gimme the Heathbar, Paul!

PAUL. Gimme the yodels!

MAGGIE. Look, I'm not playing Paul. You're a nice guy and all, but don't fuck with my food!

PAUL. You're a Compulsive Overeater too, aren't you?!

MAGGIE. I'm gonna compulsively kick you in the fuckin' ass if you don't back away from my damn food!

PAUL. I know what you're going through.

MAGGIE. Heathbar!

PAUL. You're overloaded with shame and guilt —

MAGGIE. Step off my fuckin' food!

PAUL. — Anger, yes! — *MAGGIE!*

MAGGIE. Get outta my apartment!

PAUL. — Maggie —

MAGGIE. Get out! Call a cop, bust me, turn me in, I don't care! Just move away from the food and get out!!!

PAUL. Don't open those Yodels, Maggie! Maggie, Goddamnit! Halt! … NOW, PUT THE FUCKIN' YODELS DOWN! I'm not letting you eat them for two reasons: number one, they're stolen; and me and you are gonna gather all this stuff up and return it. All of it! Because that is how the program works. You called me tonight because you knew you had to reach out and that you had to return the stuff and make amends with the storekeeper. *Reach out and Return,* the first principle of the program. You called me tonight because you are brave, Maggie, you called me because you wanna turn it around. You're a winner, Maggie. You're gonna lick this, I can tell. Six months from now, you'll be leading workshops, visiting prisons, talking to youngsters at school. You'll be making a difference. Now, you could eat those Yodels and just give the guy the seventy-nine cents but I'm not going to let you do that to yourself 'cuz you're a compulsive overeater, aren't you?

MAGGIE. … I'm a compulsive everything.

PAUL. Look, you got a problem with junk food and you got a problem with larceny. You're already working on the larceny, and I'd be glad to take you to an O.A. meeting.

MAGGIE. O.A.?

PAUL. Overeaters Anonymous, I'm an O.A. member.

11

MAGGIE. You don't look like no overeater.

PAUL. I used to weigh four-hundred pounds.

MAGGIE. No way.

PAUL. Here's a photo of me on a horse.

MAGGIE. Oh my God!

PAUL. Now here's a picture of that same horse ten minutes later.

MAGGIE. Is it sleeping?

PAUL. Afraid not. I look at this picture everyday to remind me of the pain and suffering, and in this case, death, that my compulsive overeating has cost myself and others … Back then, I was a mess. I smoked four packs of cigarettes a day, and when I wasn't sitting in front of the TV inhaling food, I was robbing this town blind. I was a big, fat, chain-smoking, kleptomaniac. I was miserable. I hated myself. Hated myself so much I couldn't function. Have you ever felt that way?

MAGGIE. … All the time.

PAUL. … Can I ask you something?

MAGGIE. What?

PAUL. Do you like … life?

MAGGIE. I, I don't know.

PAUL. I *like* life. I really do. I didn't always feel that way. *(Pause.)*

MAGGIE. I can't believe I stole 800 bucks from you and you're still being so nice to me.

PAUL. Hey, all you gotta do is apologize for your actions sincerely and promise to make reparations and we're square. In fact, it would be an honor to be the first person that you exercised the first principle with.

MAGGIE. Paul —

PAUL. — Just try it. *(Pause.)*

MAGGIE. Paul, I …

PAUL. You …

MAGGIE. Stole … Paul, I stole … I stole …

PAUL. 800 …

MAGGIE. Paul. I stole 800 dollars from you. I'm …

PAUL. Good. You're doing good.

MAGGIE. I'm ashamed and embarrassed and I'm very, very, very sorry and I plan to pay you back. Look: Here's four bucks: I owe you 796 dollars, okay?

PAUL. I gladly accept your apology.

MAGGIE. ... Dag! I just practiced the first principle, didn't I? *(Paul claps for Maggie.)*

PAUL. Yes you did ... Hug?

MAGGIE. Okay. *(They hug.)*

PAUL. ... How do you feel?

MAGGIE. Hungry.

PAUL. You want a banana?

MAGGIE. You got a banana?

PAUL. I always carry around a couple of bananas in case I get hungry — keeps me out of Mickey D's ... Here.

MAGGIE. Thanks.

PAUL. I think I'll have one too. *(Beat. They eat Bananas.)* You're not single, right?

MAGGIE. I broke up with my boyfriend a couple of months ago. Why?

PAUL. No, just ... conversation. Not, uh, — why'd you break up?

MAGGIE. 'Cuz he's a lying cheating drinkin' druggin' con artist.

PAUL. I see.

MAGGIE. I mean, Flaco had his good points —

PAUL. — Flock O?!

MAGGIE. It means skinny in Spanish.

PAUL. He's Latino?

MAGGIE. He thinks he is. Flaco, he's one of those spur-of-the-moment people, which is cool, if, like, you don't ever wanna make something of yourself, which, I *do* wanna make something of myself, which is why I broke up with him. I don't wanna turn into no career criminal — which is where we were headed. But, you prolly don't know nothin' about that kinda stuff, Paul.

PAUL. Whaddya mean?

MAGGIE. You know — you're, like, you know.

PAUL. I'm like what?

MAGGIE. Nah. Never mind.

PAUL. Hey, let me tell you something: Back in the day, I had mad street creds.

MAGGIE. Nah, yeah, I'm sure.

PAUL. I mean — you ever crack a safe?

MAGGIE. No. Why? Did you?

PAUL. Okay — you ever hear of Maury Handleman?

MAGGIE. Who?

PAUL. Old time safe-cracker? Used to be the leader of The Den of Thieves?

MAGGIE. Who's The Den of Thieves?

PAUL. They were the greatest non-violent Jewish crime organization of the twentieth century. Maury Handleman and his crew cracked over 200 safes in the thirties and forties without ever being caught, and without ever harming a single individual. They were so good, hardly anyone to this day even knows they existed. Maury Handleman is my grandfather.

MAGGIE. For real?

PAUL. Yup.

MAGGIE. He must be got a lot a money, huh?

PAUL. Nope — He's a locksmith in Brooklyn Heights.

MAGGIE. He's not rich?

PAUL. That's not what The Den of Thieves were about. All the money? They gave it away.

MAGGIE. What?

PAUL. Yup. Funneled it to liberal politicians to build libraries.

MAGGIE. Libraries?!

PAUL. See, The Den of Thieves were immigrants. Poor and uneducated. They wanted to build a future for their children. They knew that success could be attained through education, so they set out to improve the educational system by building more libraries in poor neighborhoods so the poor could have a chance to catch up to the rich. Anyway, once they got too old for the rigors of criminal life, they split up and opened little businesses. My grandfather became a locksmith. He taught me all of it, lock picking, safe cracking — in fact — I noticed your front door locks are pathetic. I could fix them if you'd like me to.

MAGGIE. You ever crack a safe?

PAUL. Broke into a White Castle once. Got about eighty-nine bucks and a couple hundred burgers. But, I'm all done with that now. I have my health, I have my sobriety, I'm smoke-free, drug-free, debt-free, meat, sugar, dairy, and wheat-free, and because of the program, I'm theft-free. I can honestly say I'll never go back.

MAGGIE. That's amazing Paul, really.

PAUL. ... Yeah, so ... you and this Flaco guy ... no turning back?

MAGGIE. Well, he's still having trouble getting the hint. I walked out of there two months 'go, right, but he still thinks like we're together, still follows me around, still insanely jealous, even though he's already shacked up with some other chick. He follows me around the city and if anybody even looks at me — forget it — !

PAUL. He's never hit you, has he?

MAGGIE. He's not that way. He only gets violent when he's jealous.

PAUL. Sounds like a very disturbed individual.

MAGGIE. One time, he got into a fight with this big muscle guy on Orchard Beach who was looking at me and made a comment.

PAUL. What kind of comment?

MAGGIE. Something like, "Dag, girl, you so fine, why you hangin' out with that soft faggot bitch white-boy suckah?"

PAUL. ... Ouch.

MAGGIE. This guy looked like fuckin' Arnold Schwartzenegger and Flaco's a string bean. But Flaco took him on anyway. This guy, he was beating Flaco really really bad until, all a the sudden, they were rolling around on the sand and Flaco — he pulled down the big guy's Speedo — and bit the guy's ass so hard that not only did the big guy give up, but Flaco, when he got up, he spitted pieces of the guy's ass at him as he ran away.

PAUL. Sounds like a maniac.

MAGGIE. Let's put it this way if Flaco were to walk in right now and find you here, you might be leavin' missing half your ass.
(There is a loud knock at the door.)

FLACO. Yo, mami, open up! ...

MAGGIE. Oh, shit! It's him!

PAUL. Who?

MAGGIE. Him!

PAUL. You mean, Flaco?! *(Louder knocking.)*

FLACO. Yo, I brought you a nice present! Open up!

MAGGIE. You'd better hide.

PAUL. Where?

MAGGIE. Under the table.

FLACO. I hear voices!

PAUL. You can't just introduce me as a platonic friend?

MAGGIE. You wanna take that risk?

FLACO. OPEN THE FUCKIN' DOOR!!!

PAUL. I'll hide. But try to get rid of him fast. *(Paul hides under the table. Maggie opens door.)*

FLACO. Oh, ma Gawd! Am I glad to see you, baby!

MAGGIE. What do you want, Flaco?

FLACO. Yo, what kind of a greeting is that?

MAGGIE. Look, I was just about to go to sleep —

FLACO. — Well, wake up! We got a lot of work to do, and not much time to do it.

MAGGIE. Flaco —

FLACO. Yo! … What's that smell?!

MAGGIE. What smell? *(Flaco sniffs.)*

FLACO. Old Spice … I smell Old Spice!

MAGGIE. I don't smell anything —

FLACO. — Why your apartment smell like after-shave?!

MAGGIE. Well, the super was here yesterday —

FLACO. No, this is a fresh scent! … Yo! Whose bag is that?!

MAGGIE. What bag?

FLACO. "What bag"?! That bag right there! That "looking like a man's bag" bag!

MAGGIE. Go home Flaco; I'm not your girlfriend no more.

FLACO. You got a man in here don't you?!

MAGGIE. No.

FLACO. Deceit! You deceiting me! … Yo, Motherfucker! Come out of your hiding place! I know you're here!

MAGGIE. Get out my apartment, Flaco! *(Beat.)*

FLACO. You don't got a man in here?!

MAGGIE. No!

FLACO. Then that must be a prowler under the table. *(Flaco takes out a gun.)*

MAGGIE. Flaco!

FLACO. Get out from under that table, mothahfuckah! Are you a prowler, or are you fucking my girlfriend?!

MAGGIE. Flaco! Put that gun down!

FLACO. Identify yourself: prowler, or girlfriend fucker?! *(Paul emerges from under the table.)*

PAUL. I'm … I'm … I'm … I'm Paul Handleman, friend, not fucker! Friend. Gay friend. Harmless impotent gay friend!

FLACO. What are you doing here?

MAGGIE. Flaco!

PAUL. No, that's okay, Maggie. I'm here v-v-visiting. From Schenectady. That's upstate.

MAGGIE. Put that fuckin' gun away. Now! *(Flaco complies.)*

FLACO. Sorry, baby. I'm a little on edge today.

MAGGIE. What are you doing here, Flaco?

FLACO. I got news!

MAGGIE. What news?

FLACO. It's private. Tell fruit-loops to take a hike.

MAGGIE. His name is Paul Handleman, and he's staying right here.

FLACO. Who is this guy, anyway?! Yo! Who are you?!

PAUL. P-Paul Handleman.

FLACO. "Paul Handleman"?

PAUL. Paul Handleman, yes.

FLACO. … You don't look like no "Paul Handleman" to me!

PAUL. I come from an adoptive home.

FLACO. A what?!

PAUL. A-Adopted. I was adopted. I have five brothers and sisters, and they were all adopted too. My parents, they believe in adoption —

FLACO. — Well thass very fuckin' fascinating, yo, but, I got bidness to discuss with my girl here, so would you mind getting your little adopted ass outta here?

PAUL. I, I'd rather not.

FLACO. You'd rather what?!

PAUL. I, I don't feel comfortable leaving you alone with her.

FLACO. Well, maybe you'd feel more comfortable in a state of unconsciousness!

MAGGIE. Flaco, stop it! Anything you have to say to me, you can say in front of him.

FLACO. But this is bidness.

MAGGIE. I'm not in "bidness" anymore.

FLACO. Yo, this orphan boy don't look like no maricon from upstate! You fucking him, ain't you?!

MAGGIE. You're with that puta-stripper air-head bitch; why you care who I'm with?

FLACO. *So you are fucking him!*

17

PAUL. No fucking! Zero! None!

MAGGIE. I'm not with him, Flaco.

FLACO. But you'd like to be, right?!

MAGGIE. Flaco …

FLACO. Who the fuck is this guy?! What's he doing here?!

PAUL. I, I'm her sponsor.

FLACO. Sponsor? What's a sponsor?

PAUL. Maggie's in a twelve-step program for recovering thieves — I'm helping her to recover.

FLACO. Recover what?

MAGGIE. My life, I'm trying to get my life back Flaco. Paul is helping me.

FLACO. What's wrong with your life?

MAGGIE. It sucks. My life sucks!

FLACO. And that's *my* fault?!

MAGGIE. I'm trying to change my life Flaco!

FLACO. You wanna change your life? Well, that's why I came over here, baby! I got something to tell you I guarantee it's gonna change your life — but I can't say it in front of him.

MAGGIE. Why not?

FLACO. It involves, you know, a little bidness.

PAUL. "Criminal" business?

FLACO. Am I talking to you?

PAUL. Maggie let's go. You don't need this element in your life.

FLACO. What'd you call me?! An "element"?!

PAUL. I'm leaving now, Maggie. As your Sponsor, I strongly suggest you don't stay here alone. We can catch a nine o'clock meeting if we leave right now.

FLACO. Yo, Maggie. Don't listen to this little pigeon. He's trying to brainwash you. I been in rehab. It's all about that. They just wanna make you safe, so you're not a threat to them. Look at this stupid ass clown face clown. He probably never committed a felony in his life. What he know about crime?

PAUL. I know a lot about crime. Probably a lot more than you.

FLACO. Yeah right, Bozo. So lissen, Maggie —

PAUL. — You ever crack a safe?!

FLACO. No, Mr. Clown Head, I have never cracked a safe. Why? Have you?

PAUL. As a matter of fact I have.

FLACO. Get the fuck outta here.

MAGGIE. Actually, he has, Flaco.

FLACO. Nah, Serious?

PAUL. That's right.

FLACO. You know how to crack safes?

PAUL. I said yes.

FLACO. For Real? … Oh, my God! This is, this is like an omen! Sit down, both of you!

MAGGIE. We're leaving.

FLACO. Yo. You won't wanna leave after you hear what I gotta say.

MAGGIE. Flaco, whatever you're up to —

FLACO. — Up to? Up to? Why you always gotta think I'm up to something? I'm about to change your lives, yo! I'm offering you a way out.

MAGGIE. Of what?

FLACO. Poverty. Low-income housing. All a that! I'm talking 'bout the future, mami. I'm talking easy street. I'm talking about a nest egg that's gonna hatch into economic independence!

MAGGIE. You smoked some of that crack before you got here, didn't you?

PAUL. Nice meeting you, "Flaco." C'mon Maggie, grab your coat —

FLACO. SEVEN HUNDRED AND FIFTY THOUSAND DOLLARS! SEVEN HUNDRED AND FIFTY FUCKIN' THOUSAND DOLLARS, YO! Y'ALL GONNA WALK OUT ON DAT?!

MAGGIE. You're pathetic and sad, Flaco. I pray you find help … Let's go, Paul. *(Beat.)*

PAUL. … 750,000 dollars?

MAGGIE. Paul?

PAUL. … Where is this 750,000 dollars?

FLACO. Yo, before I say anything, son, you gotta prove to me that you can crack a safe.

PAUL. Fine. Have you got a safe on you?

FLACO. No.

PAUL. Then I can't prove it. How do you know the money's there?

FLACO. I know somebody in the place.

MAGGIE. Paul!

PAUL. Maggie, I'm not gonna do anything. I'm just talking.

FLACO. Yeah, we just talking.

PAUL. What kind of place is this?

FLACO. Disco. In Tribeca.

PAUL. 750,000 dollars in a disco?

FLACO. It's a *V.I.P.* disco, yo. Leonardo da Vinci hang out there and shit!

PAUL. Who?

FLACO. "Titanic," mothahfuckah?! You don't watch movies? Yo, Maggie, close the front door! You want everyone in the building to know our bidness?

MAGGIE. This isn't our "bidness." It's your "bidness."

FLACO. Listen, can I talk for a minute? Can I break this down for you?

MAGGIE. We're not interested.

PAUL. Maybe we should hear him out.

MAGGIE. Paul, I thought you swore off a life of crime.

PAUL. I did, I did. But 750,000 dollars!

MAGGIE. You'd trade in all the work you've done on yourself for a slice of 750,000 dollars?

PAUL. I'm not saying definitely. I'm just saying, let's hear him out.

MAGGIE. This shit is fucked up, Flaco! You robbed my youth, my heart, my womanly virtue, now you gonna come in here and try to rob my sponsor?! For some bullshit that you know is bullshit?!

FLACO. Yo, this ain't no bullshit, Maggie. I ain't trying to sell you no dream. This is real. This shit's a limited one-time offer. This job, this place — it's criminal how badly they're protecting that money. And you know why? 'Cuz they don't care. They make so much money, that money's like nothing to them, but for us, it's everything. You could do anything you wanted with that money. Buy a car, go to California, go to school, open up a flower store, whatever you want. Just a couple hours work and you're money troubles are *over,* baby. O-V-R-E! We'll all be home free. You too, Handlebag.

PAUL. Handleman.

FLACO. Yeah, whatever.

PAUL. Okay. Let's hear it.

MAGGIE. Paul! You've been theft-free for 682 days!

PAUL. Maggie, recovery is about "Progress, not Perfection." It's in the Big Book, you can look it up.

MAGGIE. First of all, whatever he's gonna tell us is probably bullshit anyway.

FLACO. Maggie, I've never been more honest in my life. For real! But we gotta do this by midnight 'cuz someone's coming over there to pick up the money.

PAUL. Who?

FLACO. Some European motherfuckers. Will you just hear me out?

PAUL. C'mon, Maggie, hear him out.

FLACO. Check this out: my friend, Raheem, right? He got a friend, who got a friend, who sell crack to this punk who works at this club, right? It's a big fuckin' disco called Epiphany. So I go down there, right, to meet this punk, maybe I can sell him some product. I meet him, he starts buying from me — thinks he's getting a better deal with me, which he's not — Anyway, I always meet him in this back room office on the ground floor which has an outside entrance. So I hang there, do a deal, watch some Knicks wit' him; I notice they got a *safe*. So I start coolin' with the kid on the regular, know what I'm sayin, and he's at work, but all his job requires is for him to hang in this office. I'm curious. So I befriend the motherfucker and within a week — he's kickin' it all to me! ... Turns out the club is selling mad drugs; yo, hallucinogens, speed, X — they're raking it in. And all the drug money goes in this basement safe. Someone comes to pick it up every couple of days. They send the money to, like, Sweden, or some shit. The rest, they roll over to get more product. But here's the thing. They're an independent operation! They ain't paying no one off: no Mafia, no cops no gangs, no no-one! Nobody know shit about it! I mean, it's gonna be all over for them in a couple of weeks. But meantime, they got *money* down there. 750,000 dollars. Someone's coming to pick it up at midnight, which means we got three hours to get there first. Once we've stolen it, no one will care. We're not stealing from cops or mob — there's no reason for them to know or care what we do. And the disco can't say *shit* to anyone because they'll be slaughtered if any of the heavy hitters ever know how much cash they baggin' without paying off. This is a gift from *God,* yo!

PAUL. Are you sure they're not connected?

FLACO. Point of fact, son.

PAUL. So what do you need me for?

FLACO. I need someone who can get in a safe. I was supposed to hook this job a week ago, but the guy I know who does safes was out of town. I've been pagin' him all day. He's still out of town. If Maggie vouches for you, then you're okay with me.

PAUL. How do we get in?

FLACO. Simple. I stole a key yesterday. I meet him, get him to take a walk. Keep him out about twenty minutes. You go in, hit the safe, get the money. I'll meet you back here.

PAUL. Can you get him to go out?

FLACO. This kid's a fuckin' crack-head, yo. He'd stick Cheerios up his ass and sing "La Bamba" if I tol' him to.

PAUL. How about lookouts?

FLACO. Maggie stands outside the outside door. This girl, Boochie, guards the inside door, which leads into the club. But, I'm telling you, no one else goes down there. But just in case, I'm giving this girl Boochie a gun.

PAUL. No guns!

FLACO. Fuck you mean, no guns?

PAUL. I mean no guns! If we can't do this non-violently, I won't participate.

FLACO. Yo, we ain't doin' this without pieces, yo. We gotta have guns!

PAUL. Okay. Find another safecracker.

FLACO. Yo! We won't have to *use* the guns.

MAGGIE. Then why bring them?

FLACO. Yo, you guys are crazy!

MAGGIE. No guns, Flaco!

FLACO. But —

PAUL. — No guns!

FLACO. It's just —

MAGGIE. — No guns!

FLACO. Fine! No guns! No fuckin' guns! All right?! You fuckin' happy?!

PAUL. ... Who's Boochie?

FLACO. A friend.

MAGGIE. She's his new ho!

FLACO. That ain't my girl, I told you that. Yo, I believe in second chances, mami. I'll give you yours whenever you could handle it.

PAUL. How're we splitting the money?

FLACO. We could discuss that later.

MAGGIE. No. Now!

FLACO. Okay fine. 300 grand for me, 150 each for the three of you equals 750.

PAUL. You must be joking.

FLACO. Yo, I'm the leader, son! I found it, I planned it, I'm the most visible suspect, I'm taking the biggest risk. 300 grand for me — and I'm doin' y'all a favor!

PAUL. Forget it. I'm out.

MAGGIE. Me too.

PAUL. I don't know what came over me. I'm retired. I'm 682 days theft-free. I'm outta here.

FLACO. Yo! You never heard of negotiating?

PAUL. My *soul* is not negotiable. *(Paul starts to leave.)*

FLACO. Okay okay, you little dick! What'd you have in mind?

PAUL. Nothing.

FLACO. C'mon, just give me a figure.

PAUL. You're not gonna like it.

FLACO. Try me.

PAUL. Number One, take out your gun and put it on the table.

FLACO. Yeah, right.

PAUL. You wanna make money tonight? Put the gun on the table. *(Flaco very reluctantly complies.)* I'm taking this gun and throwing it in the sewer ... Now, here's the deal: half the money goes to charity.

FLACO. Charity?! As in, like, what: "Give the money away" charity?!

PAUL. 375,000 dollars goes towards building a new library right here in this neighborhood. A place where kids can read and learn without bullets flying past their heads.

FLACO. Kids? What Kids?

PAUL. The kids in the neighborhood.

FLACO. Yo, fuck the kids! Let them build their own damn library! This ain't no fuckin' Jerry Lewis Telethon I'm runnin', mothahfuckah! Get the fuck outta here: me and Maggie gonna go find a real safecracker! Right, Maggie?

MAGGIE. If Paul's out, I'm out.

FLACO. Oh ma Gawd! Betrayal! I can't believe you sidin' with him! Thass a dagger in my heart, baby —

MAGGIE. — I'd feel a lot better about this, Flaco, if I thought someone else would benefit from this besides ourselves.

FLACO. Okay okay, fine!!! We'll donate some money to the damn public library! We'll send them a check for, like, 10,000 dollars, okay?!

PAUL. Look, "Flaco," I have a family history of criminal philanthropy to uphold. You ever hear of The Den of Thieves?

FLACO. The who?

PAUL. The Den of Thieves were a gang who grossed over forty-million dollars and gave virtually all of it away.

FLACO. Yeah? They shoulda called themselves the Den of fuckin' Idiots!

PAUL. Well, regardless of your selfish, small minded opinion, they did a lot of good for this city. My grandfather, he was the leader of the Den of Thieves. He passed the torch to me. So basically, it comes down to this: If you wanna get that safe opened, you need me, and my price is this, 375,000 dollars to charity, plus twenty-five large for me. *(Beat. Flaco smolders.)*

FLACO. … All I gotta say — Handlebush — is if you can't open that safe, it's gonna be very hazardous to the future shape of your fuckin' head.

PAUL. Have we got a deal?

FLACO. How 'bout you, Maggie? You in?

MAGGIE. Why we using your bimbo? Do you really think she has the attention span for the job?

FLACO. Listen, Boochie is very intelligent and capable. Besides, we ain't got no one else who I can trust. I trust you. I trust her. Thass it.

PAUL. What about me? You don't trust me?

FLACO. Yo. You're very lucky I need you, 'cuz if I didn't, I would smack that smirk right off your Clown Head.

PAUL. You ever been in therapy?

FLACO. You ever been in a coma? 'Cuz I'll put you there! *(A knock at the door.)*

BOOCHIE. Flaco? You in there, Flaco?

MAGGIE. Who you got knockin' at my door?

FLACO. It's Boochie — I told her to meet me here. Yo, Boochie! Come on in, it's open. *(Boochie enters in stripper gear.)*

BOOCHIE. Hey, baby!

FLACO. What are you wearing?

BOOCHIE. I just got out of work. How are you, poppi chulo?! *(Boochie surveys her surroundings.)* Dag, Flaco! This apartment — it's butt.

FLACO. Boochie, this is Maggie.

BOOCHIE. You mean, "that" Maggie?

FLACO. Yeah. Maggie, this is Boochie.

BOOCHIE. In my mind I pictured you prettier, and not tubby.

MAGGIE. Yeah? Well you're just about what I pictured.

FLACO. Ladies, ladies! Let's keep this professional. This is bidness. Let's get going. Boochie — you can change clothes on the way.

BOOCHIE. Who's this?

FLACO. That's Dick-Head; he's opening the safe.

PAUL. You know, I don't think I feel comfortable working with you. I don't trust you, and I don't think you've planned this out very carefully.

MAGGIE. Me neither.

FLACO. Damn! You people are fucked up! I go and plan a perfect robbery, yo, figure everything out to the last detail. I agree to all your ridiculous conditions, and all you do is criticize! Now listen to me. This robbery is a piece of fuckin' cake! This job is a big, red lollipop. This gonna be as easy as it gets. Retarded children could pull this off! Why? Because I have masterminded it to perfection. I've got every angle covered; every possibility accounted for, which is why I can say to you with absolute certainty, that *nothing* can go wrong. *Nothing!* The only problem we gonna have is how to spend all that cash. I guarantee we will succeed. *Only a bunch of stupid, fucking idiots could mess this up!*

ACT TWO

Scene 1

A den. Flaco, Paul, Maggie and Boochie are lined up in wooden chairs; their hands, legs, and torsos completely tied up. Bags are over their heads. After a moment, Sal enters speaking on a cell phone and carrying a large gun

SAL. *(On phone.)* This the Greek? ... Greek, hey, this is Sally 'Nads; Flat Jimmy gave me your number, said — What?! — ... The fuck you mean, "Can't take my action"? ... Joey the Turtle said what? ... Fuck the fuckin' Turtle! Lemme ax you: Do you have any idea who I am? ... Well, do you know who my Uncle is? ... Thass right, so, maybe I should just tell my *uncle,* The Big fuckin' Tuna, how you disrespect a member of his family, would you like that? ... That's What I thought —

PAUL. Help!!!

SAL. Hold on a second, Greek. *(Sal goes to Paul and shoves the gun in his mouth.)* You still there, Greek? Good. Now, gimme ten dimes each on the Rams, Jets, Chargers, Eagles, Dallas, Miami, and um ... hold on a second. *(To Paul.)* You follow football?

PAUL. Yeah?

SAL. Who you like, Bears or Lions?

PAUL. L-Lions?

SAL. Lions my ass ... *(Back on phone.)* Gimme the Bears, Greek, fifty times ... What?! Just take the fuckin' bet! And Lemme tell you this my friend: The next time you don't know who I am ... you betta know who I am! *(Louie "The Little Tuna" enters.)*

LITTLE TUNA. Who was you talkin' to Sal?

SAL. My mother.

LITTLE TUNA. That wasn't a bookie you was just talkin' to?

26

SAL. C'mon Lou, you know I don't gamble no more.

LITTLE TUNA. I hope not ... How is your mother?

SAL. She's indestructible like a — like a — thing that can't be indestructed.

LITTLE TUNA. Did you call my father yet?

SAL. Yeah.

LITTLE TUNA. What did he say?

SAL. Said he'll be back from Vegas in the morning.

LITTLE TUNA. What else did he say?

SAL. He said, "Tell the Little Tuna to *handle* it."

LITTLE TUNA. What do you think he means by that?

SAL. Bang, bang, bang. Chop, chop, chop.

LITTLE TUNA. Maybe we should just wait till he gets back.

SAL. He told you to *handle* it, Lou. Handle it means handle it. If the Big Tuna comes home and this ain't handled...?

LITTLE TUNA. You're right, Sal.

SAL. So just shoot 'em. Dinner's almost ready. *(Pause.)*

LITTLE TUNA. Ya know what? My gun, it's fucked up.

SAL. Whaddya mean?

LITTLE TUNA. I left my gun in my jeans the other night, then when the maid did the laundry, she fucked it up, so now it's all fucked up.

SAL. Use my gun.

LITTLE TUNA. Nice gun.

SAL. Thanks. *(Pause.)*

LITTLE TUNA. Sally, I don't feel like shooting nobody today.

SAL. Don't worry 'bout it, Cucino. I'll do it myself.

LITTLE TUNA. Thanks, Sal.

SAL. Go back upstairs now, play the Nintendo, I'll call you when dinner's ready.

LITTLE TUNA. Right ... Sal?

SAL. Yeah?

LITTLE TUNA. Got some broccoli in your teeth.

SAL. Oh, thanks. *(Sal cocks his gun.)*

LITTLE TUNA. So, Sal, do I know these people? Who are they?

SAL. Buncha junkies, I dunno.

LITTLE TUNA. ... Take the bags off their heads, Sal. I wanna see these losers.

27

SAL. Why should you wanna see them?

LITTLE TUNA. Just do what I say.

SAL. C'mon Louie. Don't get soft on me now.

LITTLE TUNA. Soft? You think I'm soft?

SAL. I didn't mean soft.

LITTLE TUNA. Who's the boss here, you or me?

SAL. You.

LITTLE TUNA. Say it.

SAL. Say what?

LITTLE TUNA. Say I'm the boss.

SAL. You're the boss, Lou, no questions about it.

LITTLE TUNA. Okay well, the boss says take the bags off their heads so I can see them. You got a problem with that? *(Sal takes the bags off their heads.)*

LITTLE TUNA. *Maron,* these two women were involved?

SAL. Dass right.

LITTLE TUNA. Ladies, why do you put me in this position? I don't wanna kill you. That's not my style. I prefer making love to you; wining and dining you, watching a lovely sunset over an expensive brandy with you. But you ladies, you leave me no choice. It's a good thing Sal here don't have a problem killing women.

SAL. The cross I bare.

LITTLE TUNA. *Death,* my friends, death is the sentence when you rob from Al "the Big Tuna" Pescatore, or me, "the Little Tuna"!

FLACO. We didn't know we was robbing from you.

LITTLE TUNA. Excuse me. Did you speak?

FLACO. Yes, as I was saying …

LITTLE TUNA. Stop! Sal, smack him for me … *(Sal smacks him hard.)* You don't speak! *I* speak! Get it?

FLACO. Yeah okay I …

LITTLE TUNA. Sal! Smack him. *(Sal smacks him harder.)* You don't speak. I speak, get it?

FLACO. I got it —

LITTLE TUNA. — Jesus, you're fucking dumb. Sal, box his ears.

SAL. How about I just shoot him?

LITTLE TUNA. Did I tell you to shoot him?

SAL. I'm just sayin, the quicker we shoot 'em, the quicker we can eat. I don't know about you, but I am starved over here. Ain't you starved?

LITTLE TUNA. What's for dinner?

SAL. I got a nice roast in the oven with them garlic potatoes you like.

LITTLE TUNA. Yeah? … We got enough butter?

SAL. Absolutely.

LITTLE TUNA. You sure?

SAL. It's a lock.

LITTLE TUNA. I beg you Sal: Don't tell me we got enough butter than we sit down ta eat, we ain't got enough fuckin' butter.

BOOCHIE. Please don't kill us, Sexy Mafia Man!

LITTLE TUNA. Oh! Pleading for your lives will do you no good whatsoever.

PAUL. I implore you to reconsider!

LITTLE TUNA. You *implore* me? Sal, what the fuck is this guy sayin'?

SAL. I think he's insultin' you.

LITTLE TUNA. *(Re: Maggie.)* Ah, geez, look at this one here. She's cryin' Sal.

SAL. She wasn't cryin' when she was stealin' your money.

LITTLE TUNA. You want some Kleenex, miss?

SAL. Louie —

LITTLE TUNA. Do me a favor, Sal — go buy some butter.

SAL. Louie, what the hell you doin'?

LITTLE TUNA. "What the hell am I doin'?"?! … I'll tell ya what I'm doin': Go down the Farmer's Market, Sal, pick up a pound a fuckin' butter already.

SAL. We got more than enough butter, Lou!

LITTLE TUNA. What?!

SAL. Lou —

LITTLE TUNA. — Excuse me, Sal: Do I got a sign around my neck that says, "Argue with me, I'm a fuckin' half a Mook"?!

SAL. Louie —

LITTLE TUNA. Are you Son of the Tuna, Sal?! Are you heir to the throne?! Are you?!

SAL. No.

LITTLE TUNA. Who is?

SAL. You are.

LITTLE TUNA. I am what?

SAL. Son of the Tuna, heir to the throne.

LITTLE TUNA. I like butter, Sal. I would like for there to be an abundance of butter! Now: What are you gonna do?

SAL. I'm juss sayin' —

LITTLE TUNA. Butter, Sal. Butter! Butter! Butter!

SAL. ... Can I start torturing them when I get back?

LITTLE TUNA. Fine ... Now Go. *(Sal exits.)*

BOOCHIE. I love butter, Mr. Tuna.

FLACO. Butter's great, yeah.

LITTLE TUNA. Shut up! ... Ok, Now hear me and hear me good: Against my better judgment and because I'm a compassionate kind o' fella, I'm gonna take a moment (because I'm a listener), to listen to whatever extenuating happenstances you might got to say.

FLACO.
We didn't know we were stealing from you.

PAUL.
We'd never intentionally steal from you.

BOOCHIE.
I think you're cute, Mr. Tuna.

FLACO.
It's all a big mistake.

BOOCHIE.
We'll leave town.

PAUL.
Spare us, Mr. Tuna.

FLACO.
Yo, Mr. Tuna, yo, we throw ourselves on the mercy of your court!

PAUL.
I beg of you!

LITTLE TUNA. Stop! All this begging. It's disgusting. *(To Maggie.)* You. How come you ain't debasing yourself like these other clowns? Do you speak?

MAGGIE. Yeah.

LITTLE TUNA. So, how come you're not pleading with me?

MAGGIE. You already said that we're gonna die.

LITTLE TUNA. But this is your chance to appeal.

MAGGIE. I don't wanna appeal.

LITTLE TUNA. Why not?

MAGGIE. Because you don't seem like somebody that an appeal would make any difference to.

FLACO. Yo, Mr. Tuna yo, don't listen to her! She didn't mean to make no insults about you.

LITTLE TUNA. What's your name?

FLACO. Flaco.

LITTLE TUNA. "Flock O"? Flock A' what? Flock A' fuckin'
sheeps? *(To Maggie.)* Who are you, miss?

MAGGIE. Maggie.

LITTLE TUNA. What you just said to me before, Maggie, that
was a very unfair thing ta say. But I appreciate at least you got the
balls to say it.

BOOCHIE. My name is Boochie.

LITTLE TUNA. That's nice. So, Maggie, what are you doing
with these losers?

MAGGIE. I guess I'm dying with them, aren't I?

LITTLE TUNA. Sassy! I like that. You're a very attractive woman.
Maybe we can work something out.

MAGGIE. For all of us?

LITTLE TUNA. No. For you.

MAGGIE. I'm not interested.

LITTLE TUNA. So you'd rather die than date me? That's what
you're saying?

MAGGIE. I'm saying if you kill these people, you better kill me
too. But if you let us live, I'd consider going on a date with you —
but only in a public place.

BOOCHIE. You can't do better than "consider"?! Give the man a
firm "yes"!

MAGGIE. Mr. Tuna?

LITTLE TUNA. Louie. Please.

MAGGIE. Louie, the truth is we really had no idea we were stealing from you. Flaco, he's my ex-boyfriend, he set it up and he told
us the money was clean.

FLACO. Before God, I thought it was clean!

LITTLE TUNA. Yeah, yeah, yeah. Everybody says the same shit.

FLACO. Yo, I ain't lyin' yo.

MAGGIE. Louie, he's telling the truth. He's not a liar, he's just
incredibly stupid and careless.

PAUL. I'll vouch for that.

MAGGIE. The bottom line is, we stole and we were wrong to do
it … Louie, I apologize.

PAUL. You're right, Maggie. All this begging and pleading clouded
my head from the real issue, which is stealing itself. We tried to steal
money from you, Mr. Tuna. We were wrong to do it. I apologize.

LITTLE TUNA. Apologies? This is new. Well okay: I, myself, apologize to you for having to kill youse all, but this is business. I got a reputation to uphold. Someday, I'll be a boss, and how's it gonna look if people think they can just apologize and call it a night?

MAGGIE. You're right, but do you accept our apologies?

LITTLE TUNA. Sure. Why not? Do you accept mine?

PAUL. It's just that me and Maggie, we're in a program.

LITTLE TUNA. Witness protection?

PAUL. No ... for recovering thieves. We were trying to turn our lives around.

LITTLE TUNA. Well, you fucked up.

PAUL. Yes, we did.

MAGGIE. Louie, can I ask you something?

LITTLE TUNA. Sure, honey.

MAGGIE. Didn't you ever fuck up? *(Sal enters with a chain saw.)*

SAL. Okay, let's party. *(Sal let's it rip. They all scream in terror.)*

LITTLE TUNA. Sally!

SAL. Yeah Lou?

LITTLE TUNA. Change of plans ... okay, guys, let me ask you something: Are you two in recovery also?

BOOCHIE. We're planning to enroll tomorrow.

LITTLE TUNA. Right ... Here's what's going to happen. I should not be doing this. You're very fortunate that you caught me in a moment of weakness. Maggie, you're wonderful — I'd love to date you. The rest of you, I can see that you're not really professionals. I mean, only a bunch of stupid, fucking idiots could blow a job so easy. So, out of the kindness of my heart and because somebody once spared me in a moment of weakness ...

SAL. Louie, what are you doing?

LITTLE TUNA. Sally. Go butter the roast.

SAL. Listen, your pop —

LITTLE TUNA. The roast,Sal! The fuckin' roast!

SAL. What'd these people say to you?

LITTLE TUNA. *(A warning.)* Sal —

SAL. Lou!

LITTLE TUNA. You wanna know what these fuckin' people said to me?! They said: "Sal don't seem ta lissen to a fuckin' word you say — maybe you should give Sal's job to your cousin Dino, and Sal

should go back to runnin' numbers in Miami since he loves fuckin' Spanish people and HUMIDITY so fuckin' much"! *(Sal skulks off.)* LITTLE TUNA. Now look here, I'm gonna make this short and sweet: I need one body, and three thumbs. You can decide the who's and the wherefore's among yourselves — and believe me — this is a deal you're gettin' over here! The person who dies will get two in the back of the head. Quick and painless. Maggie, I hope you live: I got two in the fifth row for Mariah Carey next week ... Anyway, at the stoke of dawn, I'll come back here with Sal. I'll expect your decision then. Goodnight. *(Louie exits Pause.)*
PAUL. "God, grant me the serenity to —
FLACO. SHUT THE FUCK UP! *(Blackout.)*

Scene 2

Maggie, Boochie, Flaco and Paul are still tied to their chairs, arguing. It is almost dawn.

BOOCHIE. — If you ask me, Paul should be the one to die!
PAUL. Why me?
BOOCHIE. 'Cuz you're fuckin' tired and annoying.
PAUL. Annoying?
BOOCHIE. Annoying!
FLACO. Amen.
PAUL. You think I'm annoying?
BOOCHIE. Are you deaf? Isn't this guy annoying?
PAUL. Even if I was annoying,which, I think that's very debatable, but even if I was, that's still no reason for me to die. Being annoying was not a capital crime the last time I checked.
FLACO. Yeah, well, it should be.
BOOCHIE. Dass right! Corny-ass scrub!
PAUL. Scrub?!
MAGGIE. Everybody stop the bullshit. That man said we had till dawn to decide who's going, and look out the window. It's almost dawn.

PAUL. I think we should just draw straws and let fate decide.

FLACO. Do you see any fuckin' straws around here?!

PAUL. No, but ...

FLACO. "But"?! But fuck you "but"! We're tied to fuckin' chairs. Even if we had straws, we couldn't draw them!

MAGGIE. Calm down, Flaco.

FLACO. Yo, he's a stupid ass. It's your fault that he's here, Maggie.

MAGGIE. It wasn't Paul who got us into this mess, Flaco.

FLACO. I didn't know it was mob money.

PAUL. You should have staked it out better. You don't just steal 750,000 dollars on a whim!

FLACO. You're a stupid little clown-faced idiot orphan clown!

PAUL. You can call me all the childish things you want to, but the bottom line is that we're in this position because of you!

BOOCHIE. Dag, Flaco, I don't wanna die.

FLACO. You're not gonna die.

PAUL. Someone's gonna die.

FLACO. Well, not me.

PAUL. How about we play a game?

FLACO. A what?!

PAUL. We'll play a game. Loser dies.

MAGGIE. What kind of game?

PAUL. How about "States and Capitals?"

BOOCHIE. How you play that?

PAUL. I name a state, you give me the state's capital. You give a state to Flaco, he gives the capital —

BOOCHIE. — I don't like that game —

FLACO. — Me neither.

PAUL. Okay how about the "Animal" game?

BOOCHIE. What's that one?

PAUL. I say an animal — for example, Aardvark. Aardvark ends with "k." You have to say an animal that starts with "k."

BOOCHIE. Like kitty cat?

PAUL. Um —

FLACO. Yo, fuck that game. *(A beat.)*

BOOCHIE. ... Paul?

PAUL. Yeah.

BOOCHIE. I'm sorry I called you annoying.

PAUL. Oh … That's nice of you to say. Apology accepted.

BOOCHIE. You're not annoying. Actually, you're kinda cute.

PAUL. Well, thank you. So are you.

BOOCHIE. Can I share something with you?

PAUL. I guess.

BOOCHIE. I think you're very philosophy.

PAUL. Philosophy?

BOOCHIE. You know, like "factual," right?

PAUL. What are you trying to say?

BOOCHIE. Factual men … make me damp.

PAUL. "Damp"?

BOOCHIE. You know, down there?

PAUL. Oh.

BOOCHIE. Paul?

PAUL. Yeah?

BOOCHIE. I'm getting kinky thoughts.

PAUL. What kind of kinky thoughts?

BOOCHIE. Kinky ones.

PAUL. Like, what?

BOOCHIE. I'm thinking about you being real heroic and volunteering to be the one who dies. Would you like to volunteer?

PAUL. Why would I volunteer?

BOOCHIE. Because if you volunteer I'll blow you.

PAUL. Blow me?

FLACO. Yo! Take my advice, it's worth it.

MAGGIE. Flaco!

BOOCHIE. Look at my lips. I got nice lips, right? Big, wet, adventurous lips. You see my tongue? I could do a lot of things with it. Look at my throat … Can you picture it, Paul? I will do it all night long. I'll be getting you so hot and I'll even do it right up to the second they pull the trigger. I'll time it so you and the gun shoot at exactly the same time … Could I ax you something, Paul?

PAUL. I guess so.

BOOCHIE. Does Paul Junior like it when he gets fondled and licked?

PAUL. Well, he don't hate it.

BOOCHIE. Ooooooooh!

PAUL. What?

BOOCHIE. I see Paul Junior and he looks very alert!

PAUL. He is not.

BOOCHIE. You like the idea to be a hero, right, Paul? Say yes, Paulie, and I'll salute you! I'll salute you like a hero should be saluted-ed.

PAUL. Look, you're not gonna seduce me so just leave me alone, okay?

BOOCHIE. ... *Maricon!*

FLACO. ... Yo, Listen up: I have an idea how we can settle this once and for all. How about each one of us take turns listing all the reasons that we want to live? Like, give a speech about it, and whoever the top three speakers are get to live.

PAUL. How're we going to judge?

FLACO. We'll vote.

BOOCHIE. *(To Flaco.)* Wait! What is this?

PAUL. Well, you see ...

BOOCHIE. *(To Paul.) Callate, pendejo! (To Flaco.)* Flaco, honey, what's going on?

PAUL. May I propose a change in the topic?

FLACO. What change?!

PAUL. Instead of listing why we would like to live, we should be listing why our loss to society would be a bad thing.

FLACO. What?!

PAUL. For example, "Society will suffer if I die because" ...

BOOCHIE. Because what?

PAUL. That's what you gotta tell us.

FLACO. I don't know about this.

MAGGIE. I think Paul's right.

FLACO. That's 'cuz you fuckin' him!

MAGGIE. I am not!

FLACO. I just think you could do better!

MAGGIE. C'mon. Let's just get this over with.

PAUL. Boochie, do you understand the criteria?

BOOCHIE. What's a criteria?

PAUL. Do you think the world will suffer if you die?

BOOCHIE. Oh, definitely.

PAUL. How about you, Flaco?

FLACO. Hell yeah. Yo, so we all agree? Who's first? *(Pause.)*

BOOCHIE. I'll go first.

FLACO. You think that's a good idea?

BOOCHIE. I'm a speak my truth.

FLACO. Good luck baby.

BOOCHIE. Thank you. *(She clears her throat.)* Society would suffer if I die for many multiples of reasons. Number one: As a exotic dancer, I bring smiles to the faces of many sad lonely mens, and sometimes womens too if they into that. Number three: I am extremely fly — as you definitely noticed — maybe in the top ten of flyest womens in the city, and if they serious about keeping New York beautiful then they gotta need me around, right? ... I'm also a sexual surrogate, which means I fuck for educationalism, which is important to society since I teach mens to fuck better, and God knows womankind could use more mens who fuck better — right, Maggie? I provide that. I also teach fellatios to the womens which I'm sure most mens could appreciate ... Number eight: I believe in charity. When I get famous, I plan on donating a lot of money to the Ronald McDonald House so sick children of all ages could always eat McDonald's for free, so even when they die, they'll die happy. Oh, also I belong in the A.S.P.C.A ... *(Pause.)* One more thing, which, I don't even know why I'm saying this,but, I got abused a lot as a child, people. A lot. And I ain't sayin' that for you to feel sorry for me,even though I wouldn't mind if you did feel sorry so I could be one a the survivors, but, the point of this is that everyone in my family called me "garbage can," including my mother, which I think dat ain't very nice, but also I think is very false 'cuz I ain't no fuckin' garbage can! And even though I gots lots and lots of talents which make me definitely a big bargain for the society, even if I didn't have *any* of those amazing skills and dreams which I, like, process — even if I *was* a garbage can — which I'm not — I'd still be valuable 'cuz where you gonna put your garbage if you don't got no can? Someone's gotta be that can, right? So, for all these ideals and many more, I feel I am a valuable ass to society and many, many peoples of all the five boroughs, and maybe even the world, would have their lives be more messed up if I wasn't around to be around ... Dass it. Thank you.

PAUL. Wow! That was really good, Boochie.

BOOCHIE. I know.

MAGGIE. Who's next?

PAUL. I'll go next.

FLACO. Oh, yeah?

PAUL. Is that okay with you?

FLACO. Yo, you wanna go next, go next.

PAUL. Okay, I will.

FLACO. But you better come up with some good shit, 'cuz if you don't, you going down!

PAUL. I'm aware of that.

FLACO. Alls I'm sayin': The pressure's on!

PAUL. I'm aware of the pressure.

FLACO. Okay, start talking.

PAUL. I will if you're through interrupting.

FLACO. Just don't choke.

PAUL. Look, why don't you go next?

FLACO. No,no! You already called it. You gotta go next or you forfeit. And if you forfeit, you lose. and if you lose, Sayonara, Mothahfucka!

PAUL. I don't like you. I wanna state that for the record.

FLACO. I don't like you either. You wanna do something about it?

PAUL. You mean fight?

FLACO. *(Mimicking Paul.)* "You mean fight?"

PAUL. Oh, mimicking. You're mimicking me! That's very clever. I'll tell you, I'm a non-violent person, but you're pushing it!

FLACO. C'mon, mothahfucka! Let's go!

MAGGIE. Flaco!

FLACO. What?

MAGGIE. This is why I left you! This is exactly why!

FLACO. What?

MAGGIE. You're tied to a chair and you want to fight. You're immobilized! Don't you realize that?!

FLACO. This guy … This fuckin' guy! He's driving me fuckin' crazy!

PAUL. *(Mimicking Flaco.)* "He's driving me crazy, he's driving me crazy"!

MAGGIE. Paul, knock it off!

BOOCHIE. Stop tormenting my man — ya big nerd-ass!

FLACO. *(To Paul.)* C'mon you little bitch! Let's hear your stupid

38

speech!

PAUL. You wanna hear a speech?! Okay, the "Little Bitch" is gonna give a speech! Deal with this! "Why Society Would Suffer If I Died" by Paul Abraham Handleman —

FLACO. — Yo, you see that?! He wasn't even listening to Boochie's speech! He was jus' pretendin' to listen, and meanwhile he was practicin' his own shit!

PAUL. That's not true!

FLACO. Paul cheated, the mothahfuckah dies! Who's wit me?

PAUL. Lemme tell you *why* society would suffer if I died, Flaco. It would suffer because, unlike you, I *contribute* to society. I am a group leader in more than a dozen 'Self Help' organizations. I don't tear down other people's self-confidence and self-esteem, I help rebuild it. Also, unlike you, "Flaco," I have a job. I pay taxes. I give to charity. I go to temple. I vote. I donate my time to volunteer agencies. I make it my responsibility to know what's going on politically. I work with children. I work with the elderly. I try to treat people with *respect* and *kindness.* Do you, Flaco? Do you do any of these things? I am trying, a day at a time, to be a good person. To "live in the solution." Now, maybe that's not "exciting" or "sexy" — maybe it's even "nerdy" — but it works for me. I am not afraid to go out and try and make a difference in this screwed up world. I say "hello" to my neighbor if I see him on the street. I lend a hand. I contribute. If nothing else, I care. I am not ashamed to say that I am a good person and that I love me and that I *care.*

FLACO. ... Is that it?

PAUL. Yes, it is.

FLACO. That sucked.

PAUL. No it didn't. Your turn, buck-o. *(Beat.)*

FLACO. ... Yeah well ... I may not be perfect. I'm man enough to admit it. I may not even be a "good" person. I might even be a "bad" person. I steal, I do crimes, I deal a little dope, I don't do any of those things you just talked about. None of them. I smoke, drink, do alotta drugs, fuckin' curse — if I see something I want, I take it. I mugged a nun once. Two nuns! ... I admit it. Up until now, I've been pretty selfish and bad — and I don't apologize for it! 'Cuz if you grew up how I did, you might be the same, maybe worse. You might be dead right now. Maybe I didn't have the opportunities you had growing up, but I ain't making excuses. I take full responsibility for who I am. I did what I thought I had to do and here I am, still alive, still standing … That's right. I am standing here with the one gift no one's ever taken away from me and no one ever will because I won't let them! I'm standin' here with a world full a *potential* still coursin' through my veins! Look at me. I'm young, good looking, highly intelligent, charismatic! I got charisma, baby! I'm a natural born leader, always have been. Can you deny it? I think not! I got so much potential, yo! I could be president. I could be a leader of my people. Some day soon, I'll be a force for *righteousness* and when that happens, I'll move mountains! War is coming, yo, and when it does, the good guys gonna need people like me, 'cause people like me, we're rare! You're right about one thing, Paul. Up until now I haven't done much to make a difference but my time is coming, son — my time is coming! If I die now, the world may be losing the next Che Gueverra, the next Malcolm X and shit, and they'll never even know I was here! I would hate for the world to suffer such a devastating loss, wouldn't you?! I'm a let your conscience be your guide, people. Finito!

BOOCHIE. Oh, Flaco. That was so perspirational!

FLACO. Suave, baby.

BOOCHIE. I love it when you get all serious. You're my Latin King.

FLACO. Siempre, siempre. *(Pause.)*

PAUL. Would you like some more time before you begin, Maggie?

MAGGIE. I'm not good at talking about myself.

PAUL. Maggie, you're an amazing person. There are so many reasons why society shouldn't have to suffer your loss.

MAGGIE. Like what?

BOOCHIE. No telling her! That's cheating!

MAGGIE. Look, I can't do this.

PAUL. Yes you can.

MAGGIE. I can't.

PAUL. Do you understand the consequences of not trying?

MAGGIE. What if I end up living and you die? I'll feel guilty. And what if my life goes on and I'm still depressed and unhappy and I decide one day to kill myself? I won't be able to do it because you already died, and if I kill myself that means you died need-lessly. So I think it's prolly better that I just die now. So I'm only responsible for my own life and not any of yours.

BOOCHIE. Thank you, God, thank you, God! Maggie, thank you, and, Girl, I'm sorry I said that thing about you not being pretty and being a tubby — you really ain't that fat, especially if this were the olden days. *(Pause.)*

FLACO. ... Yo, fuck this! I have an announcement to make. I volunteer to die. Tomorrow, baby, I die in your place.

MAGGIE. Flaco —

FLACO. I know I wasn't the best boyfriend, but one thing I do know is you're a special person.

BOOCHIE. Flaco, what about me?

FLACO. You're special too, baby ... Do you love me, Maggie?

MAGGIE. Stop!

FLACO. Nah, fuck stop! Do you love me?

MAGGIE. No.

FLACO. You're lyin'

MAGGIE. I am not!

FLACO. I gotta tell you something. I miss your smile. I miss wak-ing up in the middle of the night and watching you sleep. I miss that embarrassed look you get on your face when I catch you naked coming out of the shower. I miss your smell. I miss you. Do you miss me? Do you?

MAGGIE. ... Flaco, I am not a happy person. I can't remember ever being a happy person.

FLACO. You were happy with me. I know you were. And you bet-tah be happy in the future if I lay my life down for you, or else I'm a come back as a ghost and haunt your ass! I'll be, like, "Boo" 'n' shit!

MAGGIE. I've made up my mind, Flaco. You guys won the game. I lost. Fair is fair, and dass it. No mas. *(Pause.)*

PAUL. I lost the game, Maggie.

MAGGIE. No you didn't.

PAUL. Yes I did. I lied in my speech.

MAGGIE. About what?

PAUL. Everything. I don't do shit for other people.

MAGGIE. You did something for me.

PAUL. But did I do something for you 'cuz it was program, or was it because I wanted to, you know, sleep with you?

FLACO. I knew it! I knew that shit!

PAUL. It's one thing to do something when it's easy — but I don't think I've ever really stepped up when it's hard … It should be me who dies. I lied … I'm a liar. I should die. *(Pause.)*

BOOCHIE. I lied too … It's true I was abused a lot, but what I didn't say is I got a really good expensive therapist now, and she says we making a lot a positive progress.

FLACO. Fuck … That nun I mugged? I may have slapped her a little.

BOOCHIE. I stole a Rolex off a client las' week.

FLACO. Her friend? The other Nun? — I kicked her in her ass.

BOOCHIE. I'm a manipulator.

FLACO. I'm a convicted felon.

MAGGIE. I'm selfish.

FLACO. I'm a predator.

PAUL. I slept with my Aunt.

FLACO. You what?!

BOOCHIE. Paul, thass fuckin' disgusting!

PAUL. Who you talkin' to — you're a fuckin' whore!

BOOCHIE. And you're a aunt fucker!

FLACO. You're a fuckin' dick, man! A sick, aunt-fucking dick!

PAUL. I'm a dick?!

MAGGIE. Chill out!

PAUL. At least I don't go around acting like somebody I'm not, "Flocko"! I bet you can't speak two words of Spanish!

FLACO. Yeah? How much Yiddish you know, mothahfuckah?! 'Cuz I ain't never met no brother named "Paul," much less "Handlerag," or whatever the fuck name you tryin' ta call your clown-ass self!

PAUL. Punk ass White boy!

FLACO. Fake-recovered wannabe Jew!

BOOCHIE. Word!

MAGGIE. Stop it! Stop!

FLACO. Yo, Maggie —

MAGGIE. Look out the window! All of you! Look! *(They all look. Pause. Dawn. It gets quiet.)*

PAUL. Uh oh.

FLACO. … Dag.

BOOCHIE. … Them birds be chirpin'.

PAUL. … Yup.

FLACO. Stupid birds … I don't like birds.

BOOCHIE. Birds is nice, Flaco. What's wrong wit' birds?

FLACO. I dunno … Nuthin' I guess. *(Pause.)*

PAUL. … I had a bird once. Melvin. He used to like to eat cotton balls.

FLACO. Gee, what an inneresting fact.

MAGGIE. Flaco —

FLACO. Sorry. *(Beat.)*

MAGGIE. You really love me, Flaco?

FLACO. Like I know my own name.

MAGGIE. Let me go. I'm a sad, fearful person. I hurt people because of it.

FLACO. No you don't —

MAGGIE. I tried to hurt myself last month —

FLACO. — You what?

MAGGIE. I got scared at the last minute, but I know I'm gonna try it again, 'cuz this feeling in me — it ain't changed since as long as I can remember. That's the real truth. It's dawn. It's time. *(Lights fade.)*

Scene 3

The den. Dawn. Maggie, Flaco, Paul, and Boochie are being held at gunpoint by Sal. The Little Tuna enters:

LITTLE TUNA. *(Yawning.)* Sally, you put the coffee on?

SAL. It's percolatin'

LITTLE TUNA. Good.

SAL. I made those nice Belgian waffles, too; with the country sausages you like.

LITTLE TUNA. Are they plump?

SAL. What?

LITTLE TUNA. The sausages. You know I like 'em plump.

SAL. They're very plump.

LITTLE TUNA. Did you get the donuts?

SAL. Yeah.

LITTLE TUNA. Assorted flavors?

SAL. I told them "gimme two of everything."

LITTLE TUNA. Good man. Sally, bring out the donuts. Our guests are hungry.

SAL. Louie, these are the *good* donuts from the *good* place. You sure you wanna waste them on these guys?

LITTLE TUNA. C'mon, these people, they're probably starvin'.

SAL. So, shoot 'em. They won't be hungry no more.

LITTLE TUNA. Sally?! Is this how you wanna start the mornin'?

SAL. I'm just sayin' —

LITTLE TUNA. — Fuckin' donuts, fuckin' now! *(Sal exits.)* Good morning … Now let me start by telling you that I did a little research last night. I got information on all of you, and it pains me to have to do what I gotta do because I can see from my informants that you're all a bunch of very low-level criminals at best, and a bunch of pathetic, harmless losers at worst. Maggie, I got a hold of your school records. It seems that you are a classic under-achiever. High test scores and poor grades. I'm disappointed in you. *(Sal reenters.)*

SAL. Fresh donuts, boss.

LITTLE TUNA. Gimme the tray. *(Little Tuna grabs a donut for himself and offers the tray to Boochie.)* Have a donut.

BOOCHIE. I'd rather have something else.

LITTLE TUNA. like what?

BOOCHIE. Something "Italian."

LITTLE TUNA. You mean, like, a canoli?

BOOCHIE. Yeah, I want your canoli, Mr. Tuna!

LITTLE TUNA. My canoli? Hey! Eat a donut and forget about that shit! *(To Flaco.)* Hey you, tough guy, take a donut.

FLACO. Thanks, yo.

LITTLE TUNA. Not that one.

FLACO. Oh. *(Flaco shuffles through the donuts, poking and examining them.)*

LITTLE TUNA. Hey! What are you doin'?!

FLACO. Looking for a custard one.

LITTLE TUNA. Sal! Shoot him! *(Sal fires an errant shot.)* Whoa, whoa, I was just kidding! Hey kid, it gets me upset when people put their fingers all over all the donuts like that. Here, take this one.

FLACO. Thanks, Mr. Tuna …

LITTLE TUNA. Maggie. You can have any donut you like. How 'bout this nice Boston cream?

MAGGIE. Sure.

PAUL. Umm, Maggie?

MAGGIE. What?

PAUL. You're not gonna eat that, are you?

MAGGIE. Why not?

PAUL. Refined sugar, Maggie. That's a no-no.

LITTLE TUNA. Hey, you! Shaddup!

PAUL. Maggie. *(Pause.)*

MAGGIE. Sorry Louie, I can't eat it.

LITTLE TUNA. Why not?

PAUL. Maggie's a compulsive overeater.

LITTLE TUNA. A what?

PAUL. She eats to bury her pain … Um, you look like you might be a compulsive overeater too, if you don't mind me saying so.

LITTLE TUNA. You tryin' to say I'm overweight?

PAUL. Not at all. Just that you eat to bury your pain. Like, for instance, right now, you don't wanna kill us. It's causing you pain. So instead, you eat.

LITTLE TUNA. So you sayin' I'm fat?

FLACO. Yo, Mr. Tuna. Don't listen to this idiot. You're very trim. Believe me.

PAUL. See, Mr. Tuna! You're eating! You're burying your pain.

LITTLE TUNA. I'm gonna bury you in about a minute —

PAUL. Put the donut down, Louie!

LITTLE TUNA. What?!

MAGGIE. Paul. Stop it!

PAUL. It's okay, Maggie. Lou, you don't wanna eat that donut.

LITTLE TUNA. Why not?

PAUL. Because "there is no chemical solution to a spiritual problem."

LITTLE TUNA. Yeah? Well there is a violent solution to an

annoying problem. Sal, give me the gun. I'll shoot him myself.

PAUL. Mr. Tuna, you can shoot me, but it won't solve your problem. The first step in overcoming problems is to admit them. You're a compulsive overeater.

LITTLE TUNA. I am not!

PAUL. Mr. Tuna. I'm a compulsive overeater. You got all the symptoms.

LITTLE TUNA. You're a compulsive overeater?

PAUL. Yes, I am.

LITTLE TUNA. ... So, you don't eat donuts?

PAUL. Not for 994 days.

LITTLE TUNA. ... What would happen if you ate a donut now?

PAUL. I wouldn't eat one.

LITTLE TUNA. But, say if you did.

PAUL. Well, it would probably be a very painful experience.

LITTLE TUNA. Why?

PAUL. Look, why don't we all just go to a meeting right now? You could learn all about it.

BOOCHIE. I'm up for that!

FLACO. Me too!

LITTLE TUNA. I got a better idea. *(To Paul.)* Eat a donut right now.

PAUL. What?

LITTLE TUNA. Here. Eat it.

PAUL. I can't.

LITTLE TUNA. Eat it or I'll shoot you.

PAUL. I don't believe you.

LITTLE TUNA. Sal, take the gun. Do you believe that Sal will shoot you?!

PAUL. Okay, okay, I'll eat it.

LITTLE TUNA. Eat the whole tray! ... Sally, if he stops eating, you start shooting.

SAL. Eat! Eat!

LITTLE TUNA. Gimme one of those. *(Louie takes another donut.)* All right, let's get this over with. Who's dyin' over here?

MAGGIE. Me.

LITTLE TUNA. You! Why you?

MAGGIE. It was my decision.

LITTLE TUNA. You sure you don't wanna change your n̖
'Cuz I'll just shoot someone else, like him!
FLACO. Do what you gotta do, you compulsive overeater, you
LITTLE TUNA. Just say the word and you'll live.
MAGGIE. I can't. I won't.
LITTLE TUNA. Maggie, I like you. I don't know what it is, I don't even know you, but for some strange reason, I can't bear to shoot you.
SAL. You don't have to shoot her. I'll shoot her.
LITTLE TUNA. I know, but still, I'll feel weird about it.
PAUL. Why don't you let us all go? It's because you're a good person that you don't wanna kill her! It's because you're not an animal! You have a conscience!
LITTLE TUNA. Hey you, keep eating!
PAUL. You have a chance here to take a giant step towards redemption. You know, they have support groups for people like you. There's a guy in my Thursday group therapy belongs to a Cosa Nostra twelve-step, I could introduce you.
SAL. Please lemme shoot him! —
PAUL. — You're in denial, Mr. Tuna!
LITTLE TUNA. After we shoot Maggie, I'm gonna stab you! Repeatedly!
FLACO. Yo, Mr. Tuna, Don't take Maggie. Take me.
BOOCHIE. No! Flaco!
FLACO. I'm sorry, baby, but that's how it's gonna be.
LITTLE TUNA. No. We're gonna do this how Maggie wants it. Sal, put her in the chair … *(To Maggie.)* … You sure you don't want a donut, sweetheart?
MAGGIE. Just do it.
LITTLE TUNA. All right. God be with you and all a that. Sal: Do the job. *(The door swings open. Alphonse "The Big Tuna" Pescatore enters with luggage.)*
BIG TUNA. Hey, knock it off! That's a floor-length mink rug you're shooting her on. I mean, my carpet cleaner is good, but he's not a fuckin' magician. Louie, who the fuck are these people?
LITTLE TUNA. They're the people from the robbery, Pop.
BIG TUNA. These are the people from the robbery?
LITTLE TUNA. Yeah.

47

BIG TUNA. Then, why the fuck are they still alive? Jesus! I can't even leave you alone for the weekend.

LITTLE TUNA. I'm sorry.

BIG TUNA. C'mere, Louie.

LITTLE TUNA. OW!

BIG TUNA. This place is a fuckin' mess. What, have you been partying all week while I've been away?

LITTLE TUNA. No, Pop.

BIG TUNA. Sal! You were supposed to take care of him.

SAL. OW!

BIG TUNA. I hope you weren't at the track this weekend 'cuz Joey the Turtle says he saw you there.

SAL. The Turtle's a liar! I swear Uncle Al, I don't gamble no more.

BIG TUNA. How come I have to come home after a long hard weekend and find these people in my living room Sal, when they shoulda been dead yesterday?

SAL. Louie didn't wanna shoot nobody 'cuz he's a fuckin' homo!

(Beat.)

BIG TUNA. Louis, I'm very disappointed in you. Go take these people out back and shoot them. And when you get back, me and you are going to have a long talk.

LITTLE TUNA. Pop, I can't shoot them.

BIG TUNA. Why not?

LITTLE TUNA. I told them I'd only kill one.

BIG TUNA. So, shoot one, let Sal shoot the rest.

LITTLE TUNA. But Daddy, I made a deal with them.

BIG TUNA. You made a deal?

LITTLE TUNA. Yeah.

BIG TUNA. Spare three, shoot one?

LITTLE TUNA. Yeah.

BIG TUNA. What do you get in return?

LITTLE TUNA. I don't remember.

BIG TUNA. Well then, that's a shit deal, don't you think?

PAUL. Mr. Big Tuna? I'm Paul Abraham Handleman and I'd like to say that you should be proud of your son. There are seeds of compassion and love in him.

BIG TUNA. Seeds, eh?

PAUL. That's right.

BIG TUNA. I always worried about that. He gets it from his mother.

PAUL. You should support him, not berate him.

BIG TUNA. What'd you say your name was?

PAUL. Handleman.

BIG TUNA. I knew a Handleman once. Maury Handleman.

PAUL. Yes, yes! He's my grandfather.

BIG TUNA. Grandfather? Well, knowing Maury, I ain't surprised — liberal bastard. Actually, you two got a lot in common.

PAUL. Thank you.

BIG TUNA. Yeah, He was a preachy little bastard just like you. Always saying I should give more to "charity." I don't like charity ... Maury Handleman ... what a piece of work. One time, your grandpop comes to me with this big score. He was gonna hit the Republican National Committee Campaign Fund safe. Steal all the money. He had it planned perfectly. I was impressed. I was all set to collaborate with his Den a ... What'd they call themselves?

PAUL. Den of Thieves.

BIG TUNA. Right. Den of Thieves. I was all set to do it and I axed him, "What's my cut?" "Nothing," he says. "Nothing"? He tells me we're takin' all the money to fund some book thing, a bunch of trucks with books, goin' to inner-city neighborhoods givin' out books.

PAUL. The bookmobile!

BIG TUNA. Crazy bastard. Hey, is your grandfather still alive?

PAUL. Yes, he is. He has his own locksmith shop in Brooklyn Heights.

BIG TUNA. That's terrific. I'll have to visit him sometime.

PAUL. He'd love that.

BIG TUNA. Absolutely. Okay, Sal. Take them all out back and shoot 'em!

LITTLE TUNA. Pop! You can't shoot these people.

BIG TUNA. Why not?

LITTLE TUNA. They're good people.

BIG TUNA. Son, I know what you're thinking, and it's admirable. But good people die every day. We don't know why, but they do. It's God's way.

LITTLE TUNA. But Pop, why can't we just forgive them?

49

BIG TUNA. Forgive? What's that?

LITTLE TUNA. Like the time I burned down the house; like the time I kidnapped my principal —

BIG TUNA. — I know what you're saying, but those incidents was different. You didn't steal 500 grand from me.

FLACO. 500 grand?

PAUL. Mr. Tuna, did you just say we stole 500 grand from you?

FLACO. So where's the other 250?

BIG TUNA. What are you talking about?

PAUL. There was 750,000 dollars in that safe. I opened it myself. I counted it!

BIG TUNA. Wait a second! Sal, you told me 500 large.

SAL. 'Cuz that's what it was. This kid don't know what he's talking about.

PAUL. Mr. Big Tuna, it was 750,000 dollars. I swear. I counted it. I even showed it to Maggie.

BIG TUNA. Who's Maggie?

PAUL. The girl with the blindfold.

LITTLE TUNA. Maggie, how much money was in that safe?

MAGGIE. 750,000 dollars. *(The Tuna draws his gun.)*

BIG TUNA. Where you goin' Sal?

SAL. Feed the cat.

BIG TUNA. We ain't got a cat. Son, go upstairs and check out Sal's room.

LITTLE TUNA. Okay Pop. *(Louie exits upstairs.)*

SAL. I swear to God, Uncle Al —

BIG TUNA. — Just sit tight ... So, how was the weather while I was away?

BOOCHIE. Very pleasant, Mr. Tuna.

BIG TUNA. What's your name?

BOOCHIE. Boochie.

BIG TUNA. You gotta nice rack, Boochie.

BOOCHIE. I know. *(Louie reenters.)*

BIG TUNA. What is it, son? What'd you find?

LITTLE TUNA. 250,000 cash and a John Holmes blowup doll.

SAL. The doll ain't mine, it's for a friend.

BIG TUNA. This upsets me, Sal.

SAL. I know ... I'm upset too.

BIG TUNA. I don't know how I can help you over here.

SAL. … I'm a compulsive gambler, Uncle Al, I need them twelve steps.

BIG TUNA. … You ready to take the first step?

SAL. Sure, why not?.

BIG TUNA. Step One: Die! *(Big Tuna shoots Sal dead.)* I didn't have a choice, son.

LITTLE TUNA. I know Pop —

BIG TUNA. Get him up before he ruins the carpet … It looks like you people saved me a lot of money. I'm gonna do you a favor. Everybody, give me a thumb, we'll call it even.

LITTLE TUNA. C'mon, Pop. Don't be cheap. These people just made us an extra 250,000 we didn't even know we had. No thumbs.

BIG TUNA. All right, all right. No thumbs. Christ. Beat it, all of you … Son, Gimme a donut.

LITTLE TUNA. Here, Pop.

BIG TUNA. Have one too, son.

LITTLE TUNA. … I can't.

BIG TUNA. Why not?

LITTLE TUNA. I think I'm a compulsive overeater.

PAUL. Bravo Lou!

BIG TUNA. A what?

LITTLE TUNA. Pop. I eat to bury my pain.

BIG TUNA. What pain?

LITTLE TUNA. I got pain Pop. Pain all over.

BIG TUNA. Your girlfriend beating on you again?

LITTLE TUNA. Not that kind of pain, Pop.

BIG TUNA. What's the problem, son? *(Pause.)*

LITTLE TUNA. I, I don't think I wanna be a wiseguy no more, Pop. I'm not cut out for it.

BIG TUNA. … Gimme another donut, son.

LITTLE TUNA. You see?

BIG TUNA. You see, what?

LITTLE TUNA. You're a compulsive overeater too.

BIG TUNA. Who's puttin' this crap in your head, son?

LITTLE TUNA. These guys. These two over here are compulsive overeaters and compulsive thieves. They're in some kind of recovery program.

BIG TUNA. What about you? You in recovery too?

BOOCHIE. No, Mr. Tuna. I'm in un-covery.

BIG TUNA. I like her. *(To Flaco.)* What about you?

FLACO. Well, Mr. Tuna … can I call you Al?

BIG TUNA. No!

FLACO. Okay, well, I don't believe in all this recovery shit.

BIG TUNA. Me neither.

FLACO. I think it's a government conspiracy to turn everybody soft.

BIG TUNA. Now here's a man with a head on his shoulders.

FLACO. But —

BIG TUNA. What but?

FLACO. But Maggie, she's my girl. Well, ex-girl.

BIG TUNA. Who's Maggie?

LITTLE TUNA. Over here Pop.

FLACO. I'm in love with Maggie, Mr. Tuna. So, even though I think this crap is a load of crap, I'd be willing to give it a shot if she'd take me back.

MAGGIE. You would?

FLACO. I was thinkin' maybe I'd get a legit job. Like a bookie, or something.

MAGGIE. Flaco.

FLACO. Did I say bookie? I meant busboy.

BIG TUNA. You'd be a busboy for this girl?

FLACO. If I had to, yeah.

MAGGIE. You could go back to school, Flaco.

FLACO. That's an idea. I'll get my grammar-school equivalency and take it from there.

BIG TUNA. This is very touching, over here. *(To Louie.)* So, son, you want out, eh?

LITTLE TUNA. Yeah, Daddy, I do.

BIG TUNA. You wanna go back to school too?

LITTLE TUNA. Sure, why not?

BIG TUNA. I'll call Yale. We got friends in the New Haven area. You could start next week.

LITTLE TUNA. I was thinking about goin' to a meeting with these guys. Is that Okay?

BIG TUNA. Do what you gotta do, son.

LITTLE TUNA. You wanna come too, Pop?

PAUL. That's a great idea.

BIG TUNA. Don't push your luck, Handleman. *(Beat. Big Tuna grabs another donut.)* You kids today, you baffle me with your problems. Nah, really, I'm standing here in a state of bafflement. You think we didn't have problems in the old days?

LITTLE TUNA. We know you did, Pop.

BIG TUNA. Forget about it. Our problems made your problems look fuckin' ridiculous! When I was you people's age, I had three paper routes, I drove a fruit truck, worked part-time at the barbershop — all those jobs I did before noon. Then I went to the trade school. Took classes, got out of school, worked at your Uncle Marco's restaurant till midnight, went home, slept three hours and did it all over again. One day I says to your Grandpa Pepe, "This is too much for me. I got unhappy problems. Life's getting me down." You know what Granpa Pepe said to me?

LITTLE TUNA. Was it —

BIG TUNA. — Grandpa Pepe said to me — I'll never forget it — "Life … is like an artichoke."

BOOCHIE. An artichoke?

BIG TUNA. That's right, honey. See, an artichoke's got the sweet meat inside. But it's small. The rest of the artichoke, you can't do nothin' wit' it. Anyways, Grandpa Pepe, he says; "Life is like an artichoke: you take the sweet meat. The rest? You throw it away." Now, that's what you young people gotta friggin' learn.

PAUL. … So, that helped you out?

BIG TUNA. Yeah, that and the fact that I turned to crime. The two of them — they made my life a lot better.

FLACO. Great story, Mr. Tuna.

PAUL. I disagree.

BIG TUNA. Excuse me?

MAGGIE. Paul —

PAUL. — No disrespect Mr. Tuna, but life is *not* like an artichoke.

MAGGIE. Paul —

PAUL. And even if it was, people are not capable of simply throwing away all the bad stuff that happens to them! That's why we live in a nation filled with abusers and addicts, because people like Grandpa Fuckin' Pepe tell us we're *not supposed* to dwell on the bad things, and that we *should be able* to just hang on to the good things, and that makes us feel guilty for even acknowledging our pain; it makes us feel inadequate that we can't just block it out, so we bury it; and replace honesty with lies, humility with self importance, and love of God with hatred of self!

FLACO. *(To Big Tuna, re: Paul.)* I don't know this guy!

BIG TUNA. You finished, Handleman?

PAUL. You just killed your own nephew! You think you're gonna be able to just throw away that part of the artichoke, "Al"?!

LITTLE TUNA. Pop, remember your blood pressure —

FLACO. *(To Paul.)* You are seriously a demented retart!

MAGGIE. — Paul, it's time to go

PAUL. I'm just trying to carry the message to those who still suffer!

BIG TUNA. Son, why don't you take your new friends out to breakfast?

LITTLE TUNA. Sure thing, pop.

BIG TUNA. *(Re: Paul.)* Not him! Me and Paulie here are gonna have a little pow wow.

LITTLE TUNA. Pop —

BIG TUNA. It was nice meeting youse people. Maggie, if this guy gives you any problems, you give me a call.

MAGGIE. Thanks, Mr. Tuna.

FLACO. Mr. Tuna, can I have your autograph? I've followed all your trials in the papers, I'm a big fan

BIG TUNA. Sure kid. Here you go.

BOOCHIE. Bye, Mr. Sexy Tuna

BIG TUNA. I'll see you again, Lamb Chop. *(Little Tuna tries to embrace Big Tuna.)*

LITTLE TUNA. I love you, pop. *(Big Tuna fishes for car keys.)*

BIG TUNA. … Here. Take the Lexus, but don't fuck it up. *(They exit. Beat.)*

PAUL. Mr. Tuna sir, perhaps I was a little inappropriate a moment ago, taking your inventory like that, and I just want to seize this opportunity to beg your forgiveness, because, the fact is, I have a very low tolerance for pain and —

BIG TUNA. Step One: We admitted that we were powerless over alcohol — that our lives had become unmanageable. Two: Came to believe —

PAUL. You're in program?

BIG TUNA. Twenty years. I'm an alcoholic.

PAUL. I thought you looked familiar!

BIG TUNA. Shaddup! ... I killed my nephew out of anger and I'm gonna have to live with that, but the fact is that he was a hopeless degenerate gambler and I took him out of his misery, and I'm sure that if I had prayed about it first, that the Higher Power of My Understanding woulda okayed the hit.

PAUL. If you say so.

BIG TUNA. I do say so! Now let's talk about you. You stole money from me and you disrespected me in front of my son. What do you think you should do about that?

PAUL. I need to make a coupla amends to you.

BIG TUNA. Did you see my property on your way in here last night?

PAUL. Very impressive.

BIG TUNA. We like it. I got my own forest out back, fifty acres.

PAUL. Wow.

BIG TUNA. My gardener's on vacation, so I want you to mow the forest for me.

PAUL. Mow the forest?

BIG TUNA. The forest, yes. Make it nice. That's amend number one ... Amend number two is I want you to sponsor my son in that overeater program. You got balls, Handleman, and you got the strength of your convictions. I admire that in a man. Now, go out back and start mowing my forest, and when you finish sometime next month, come back and see me and we'll talk about sugar 'n' spice and everything like that.

PAUL. Sugar and spice?

BIG TUNA. To the forest, Handleman. Now!

PAUL. Yes, sir. Thank you sir. *(Paul exits. A beat. Boochie enters.)*

BOOCHIE. Mr. Tuna?

BIG TUNA. Boochie, what are you doin' over here?

BOOCHIE. I thought you might like some friendly company. *(Boochie takes off her coat.)*

BIG TUNA. My God, you were built for lovin', weren't you?

BOOCHIE. Uh-huh

BIG TUNA. C'mere *(They embrace.) Maron!* You're a hot tamale!

BOOCHIE. And you're a big calzoney, Mr. Tuna

BIG TUNA. Al.

BOOCHIE. Al.

BIG TUNA. Lemme ax you something, Boochie You like diamonds and furs and a life of extravagant leisure?

BOOCHIE. Yeah. You like fellatios?

BIG TUNA. … I think we're gonna get along fine. *(Lights fade.)*

End of Play

PROPERTY LIST

Handbag (MAGGIE)
Yodels (MAGGIE)
Toothpaste (MAGGIE)
Parmesan cheese (MAGGIE)
Pesto sauce (MAGGIE)
Room freshener (MAGGIE)
Mystery fruit (MAGGIE)
2 tomatoes (MAGGIE)
Wallet (MAGGIE)
Change purse (MAGGIE)
Miscellaneous stolen goods (MAGGIE)
Four dollars (MAGGIE)
2 bananas (PAUL)
3 guns (FLACO, SAL, BIG TUNA)
Rope/twine (FLACO, PAUL, MAGGIE, BOOCHIE)
Bags (FLACO, PAUL, MAGGIE, BOOCHIE)
Cell phone (SAL)
Chain saw (SAL)
Tray of donuts (SAL)
Luggage (BIG TUNA)
Car keys (BIG TUNA)

NEW PLAYS

★ **MONTHS ON END by Craig Pospisil.** In comic scenes, one for each month of the year, we follow the intertwined worlds of a circle of friends and family whose lives are poised between happiness and heartbreak. "...a triumph...these twelve vignettes all form crucial pieces in the eternal puzzle known as human relationships, an area in which the playwright displays an assured knowledge that spans deep sorrow to unbounded happiness." –*Ann Arbor News.* "...rings with emotional truth, humor...[an] endearing contemplation on love...entertaining and satisfying." –*Oakland Press.* [5M, 5W] ISBN: 0-8222-1892-5

★ **GOOD THING by Jessica Goldberg.** Brings us into the households of John and Nancy Roy, forty-something high-school guidance counselors whose marriage has been increasingly on the rocks and Dean and Mary, recent graduates struggling to make their way in life. "...a blend of gritty social drama, poetic humor and unsubtle existential contemplation..." –*Variety.* [3M, 3W] ISBN: 0-8222-1869-0

★ **THE DEAD EYE BOY by Angus MacLachlan.** Having fallen in love at their Narcotics Anonymous meeting, Billy and Shirley-Diane are striving to overcome the past together. But their relationship is complicated by the presence of Sorin, Shirley-Diane's fourteen-year-old son, a damaged reminder of her dark past. "...a grim, insightful portrait of an unmoored family..." –*NY Times.* "MacLachlan's play isn't for the squeamish, but then, tragic stories delivered at such an unrelenting fever pitch rarely are." –*Variety.* [1M, 1W, 1 boy] ISBN: 0-8222-1844-5

★ **[SIC] by Melissa James Gibson.** In adjacent apartments three young, ambitious neighbors come together to discuss, flirt, argue, share their dreams and plan their futures with unequal degrees of deep hopefulness and abject despair. "A work...concerned with the sound and power of language..." –*NY Times.* "...a wonderfully original take on urban friendship and the comedy of manners—a *Design for Living* for our times..." –*NY Observer.* [3M, 2W] ISBN: 0-8222-1872-0

★ **LOOKING FOR NORMAL by Jane Anderson.** Roy and Irma's twenty-five-year marriage is thrown into turmoil when Roy confesses that he is actually a woman trapped in a man's body, forcing the couple to wrestle with the meaning of their marriage and the delicate dynamics of family. "Jane Anderson's bittersweet transgender domestic comedy-drama ...is thoughtful and touching and full of wit and wisdom. A real audience pleaser." –*Hollywood Reporter.* [5M, 4W] ISBN: 0-8222-1857-7

★ **ENDPAPERS by Thomas McCormack.** The regal Joshua Maynard, the old and ailing head of a mid-sized, family-owned book-publishing house in New York City, must name a successor. One faction in the house backs a smart, "pragmatic" manager, the other faction a smart, "sensitive" editor and both factions fear what the other's man could do to this house— and to them. "If Kaufman and Hart had undertaken a comedy about the publishing business, they might have written *Endpapers*...a breathlessly fast, funny, and thoughtful comedy ...keeps you amused, guessing, and often surprised...profound in its empathy for the paradoxes of human nature." –*NY Magazine.* [7M, 4W] ISBN: 0-8222-1908-5

★ **THE PAVILION by Craig Wright.** By turns poetic and comic, romantic and philosophical, this play asks old lovers to face the consequences of difficult choices made long ago. "The script's greatest strength lies in the genuineness of its feeling." –*Houston Chronicle.* "Wright's perceptive, gently witty writing makes this familiar situation fresh and thoroughly involving." –*Philadelphia Inquirer.* [2M, 1W (flexible casting)] ISBN: 0-8222-1898-4

DRAMATISTS PLAY SERVICE, INC.
440 Park Avenue South, New York, NY 10016 212-683-8960 Fax 212-213-1539
postmaster@dramatists.com www.dramatists.com

NEW PLAYS

★ **BE AGGRESSIVE by Annie Weisman.** Vista Del Sol is paradise, sandy beaches, avocado-lined streets. But for seventeen-year-old cheerleader Laura, everything changes when her mother is killed in a car crash, and she embarks on a journey to the Spirit Institute of the South where she can learn "cheer" with Bible belt intensity. "...filled with lingual gymnastics...stylized rapid-fire dialogue..." –*Variety.* "...a new, exciting, and unique voice in the American theatre..." –*BackStage West.* [1M, 4W, extras] ISBN: 0-8222-1894-1

★ **FOUR by Christopher Shinn.** Four people struggle desperately to connect in this quiet, sophisticated, moving drama. "...smart, broken-hearted...Mr. Shinn has a precocious and forgiving sense of how power shifts in the game of sexual pursuit...He promises to be a playwright to reckon with..." –*NY Times.* "A voice emerges from an American place. It's got humor, sadness and a fresh and touching rhythm that tell of the loneliness and secrets of life...[a] poetic, haunting play." –*NY Post.* [3M, 1W] ISBN: 0-8222-1850-X

★ **WONDER OF THE WORLD by David Lindsay-Abaire.** A madcap picaresque involving Niagara Falls, a lonely tour-boat captain, a pair of bickering private detectives and a husband's dirty little secret. "Exceedingly whimsical and playfully wicked. Winning and genial. A top-drawer production." –*NY Times.* "Full frontal lunacy is on display. A most assuredly fresh and hilarious tragicomedy of marital discord run amok...absolutely hysterical..." –*Variety.* [3M, 4W (doubling)] ISBN: 0-8222-1863-1

★ **QED by Peter Parnell.** Nobel Prize-winning physicist and all-around genius Richard Feynman holds forth with captivating wit and wisdom in this fascinating biographical play that originally starred Alan Alda. "QED is a seductive mix of science, human affections, moral courage, and comic eccentricity. It reflects on, among other things, death, the absence of God, travel to an unexplored country, the pleasures of drumming, and the need to know and understand." –*NY Magazine.* "Its rhythms correspond to the way that people—even geniuses—approach and avoid highly emotional issues, and it portrays Feynman with affection and awe." –*The New Yorker.* [1M, 1W] ISBN: 0-8222-1924-7

★ **UNWRAP YOUR CANDY by Doug Wright.** Alternately chilling and hilarious, this deliciously macabre collection of four bedtime tales for adults is guaranteed to keep you awake for nights on end. "Engaging and intellectually satisfying...a treat to watch." –*NY Times.* "Fiendishly clever. Mordantly funny and chilling. Doug Wright teases, freezes and zaps us." –*Village Voice.* "Four bite-size plays that bite back." –*Variety.* [flexible casting] ISBN: 0-8222-1871-2

★ **FURTHER THAN THE FURTHEST THING by Zinnie Harris.** On a remote island in the middle of the Atlantic secrets are buried. When the outside world comes calling, the islanders find their world blown apart from the inside as well as beyond. "Harris winningly produces an intimate and poetic, as well as political, family saga." –*Independent (London).* "Harris' enthralling adventure of a play marks a departure from stale, well-furrowed theatrical terrain." –*Evening Standard (London).* [3M, 2W] ISBN: 0-8222-1874-7

★ **THE DESIGNATED MOURNER by Wallace Shawn.** The story of three people living in a country where what sort of books people like to read and how they choose to amuse themselves becomes both firmly personal and unexpectedly entangled with questions of survival. "This is a playwright who does not just tell you what it is like to be arrested at night by goons or to fall morally apart and become an aimless yet weirdly contented ghost yourself. He has the originality to make you feel it." –*Times (London).* "A fascinating play with beautiful passages of writing..." –*Variety.* [2M, 1W] ISBN: 0-8222-1848-8

DRAMATISTS PLAY SERVICE, INC.
440 Park Avenue South, New York, NY 10016 212-683-8960 Fax 212-213-1539
postmaster@dramatists.com www.dramatists.com

NEW PLAYS

★ **SHEL'S SHORTS by Shel Silverstein.** Lauded poet, songwriter and author of children's books, the incomparable Shel Silverstein's short plays are deeply infused with the same wicked sense of humor that made him famous. "…[a] childlike honesty and twisted sense of humor." –*Boston Herald.* "…terse dialogue and an absurdity laced with a tang of dread give [*Shel's Shorts*] more than a trace of Samuel Beckett's comic existentialism." –*Boston Phoenix.* [flexible casting] ISBN: 0-8222-1897-6

★ **AN ADULT EVENING OF SHEL SILVERSTEIN by Shel Silverstein.** Welcome to the darkly comic world of Shel Silverstein, a world where nothing is as it seems and where the most innocent conversation can turn menacing in an instant. These ten imaginative plays vary widely in content, but the style is unmistakable. "…[*An Adult Evening*] shows off Silverstein's virtuosic gift for wordplay…[and] sends the audience out…with a clear appreciation of human nature as perverse and laughable." –*NY Times.* [flexible casting] ISBN: 0-8222-1873-9

★ **WHERE'S MY MONEY? by John Patrick Shanley.** A caustic and sardonic vivisection of the institution of marriage, laced with the author's inimitable razor-sharp wit. "…Shanley's gift for acid-laced one-liners and emotionally tumescent exchanges is certainly potent…" –*Variety.* "…lively, smart, occasionally scary and rich in reverse wisdom." –*NY Times.* [3M, 3W] ISBN: 0-8222-1865-8

★ **A FEW STOUT INDIVIDUALS by John Guare.** A wonderfully screwy comedy-drama that figures Ulysses S. Grant in the throes of writing his memoirs, surrounded by a cast of fantastical characters, including the Emperor and Empress of Japan, the opera star Adelina Patti and Mark Twain. "Guare's smarts, passion and creativity skyrocket to awesome heights…" –*Star Ledger.* "…precisely the kind of good new play that you might call an everyday miracle…every minute of it is fresh and newly alive…" –*Village Voice.* [10M, 3W] ISBN: 0-8222-1907-7

★ **BREATH, BOOM by Kia Corthron.** A look at fourteen years in the life of Prix, a Bronx native, from her ruthless girl-gang leadership at sixteen through her coming to maturity at thirty. "…vivid world, believable and eye-opening, a place worthy of a dramatic visit, where no one would want to live but many have to." –*NY Times.* "…rich with humor, terse vernacular strength and gritty detail…" –*Variety.* [1M, 9W] ISBN: 0-8222-1849-6

★ **THE LATE HENRY MOSS by Sam Shepard.** Two antagonistic brothers, Ray and Earl, are brought together after their father, Henry Moss, is found dead in his seedy New Mexico home in this classic Shepard tale. "…His singular gift has been for building mysteries out of the ordinary ingredients of American family life…" –*NY Times.* "…rich moments …Shepard finds gold." –*LA Times.* [7M, 1W] ISBN: 0-8222-1858-5

★ **THE CARPETBAGGER'S CHILDREN by Horton Foote.** One family's history spanning from the Civil War to WWII is recounted by three sisters in evocative, intertwining monologues. "…bittersweet music—[a] rhapsody of ambivalence…in its modest, garrulous way…theatrically daring." –*The New Yorker.* [3W] ISBN: 0-8222-1843-7

★ **THE NINA VARIATIONS by Steven Dietz.** In this funny, fierce and heartbreaking homage to *The Seagull*, Dietz puts Chekhov's star-crossed lovers in a room and doesn't let them out. "A perfect little jewel of a play…" –*Shepherdstown Chronicle.* "…a delightful revelation of a writer at play; and also an odd, haunting, moving theater piece of lingering beauty." –*Eastside Journal (Seattle).* [1M, 1W (flexible casting)] ISBN: 0-8222-1891-7

DRAMATISTS PLAY SERVICE, INC.
440 Park Avenue South, New York, NY 10016 212-683-8960 Fax 212-213-1539
postmaster@dramatists.com www.dramatists.com